About This Book

This book supplies twenty ready-to-use questionnaires, covering topics we have seen organizations research time and time again. We refer to them throughout this book as *quick questionnaires*. They are derived from our experience providing employee surveys since 1987. All of the items presented in these questionnaires have been used repeatedly: a large number of people have been able to read, comprehend, and respond to them. These questions are tested vehicles.

Nevertheless, your situation may call for some customized questions, either by changing the existing ones or creating new ones. To help you with this, Chapter Eight explains some basics of questionnaire development. The questionnaires are provided in hard copy as well as electronic format on the accompanying CD. You can add, exchange, and delete questions as you see fit.

Who will benefit from reading this book?

In our experience, when a workforce expands beyond about fifty people, it becomes difficult for any single individual or team to gauge the level and depth of employees' viewpoints on important organizational issues reliably. This is a point at which many management teams express the need to do systematic data gathering, such as with surveys. A human resource professional may be the point person for such surveys in medium-size businesses and a measurement specialist in larger businesses. In small businesses, an office manager, department manager, or high-level executive assistant may conduct the survey. Usually those who do this work wish they had more time, experience, or skill to do the job well.

This book will help reduce the size of the task for anyone. The advice, experience, and surveys offered are appropriate for any size and type of organization, including multinational organizations. It provides the tools that are needed to get focused information fast. The book aims to provide the inquiring management team and human resource department with flexibility and independence.

How to use this book?

Each questionnaire is printed in a copier-ready format and is also supplied on a CD in .PDF and .DOC formats. You can use them as they are or customize them using the CD version.

About Pfeiffer

Pfeiffer serves the professional development and hands-on resource needs of training and human resource practitioners and gives them products to do their jobs better. We deliver proven ideas and solutions from experts in HR development and HR management, and we offer effective and customizable tools to improve workplace performance. From novice to seasoned professional, Pfeiffer is the source you can trust to make yourself and your organization more successful.

Essential Knowledge Pfeiffer produces insightful, practical, and comprehensive materials on topics that matter the most to training and HR professionals. Our Essential Knowledge resources translate the expertise of seasoned professionals into practical, how-to guidance on critical workplace issues and problems. These resources are supported by case studies, worksheets, and job aids and are frequently supplemented with CD-ROMs, websites, and other means of making the content easier to read, understand, and use.

Essential Tools Pfeiffer's Essential Tools resources save time and expense by offering proven, ready-to-use materials—including exercises, activities, games, instruments, and assessments—for use during a training or team-learning event. These resources are frequently offered in looseleaf or CD-ROM format to facilitate copying and customization of the material.

Pfeiffer also recognizes the remarkable power of new technologies in expanding the reach and effectiveness of training. While e-hype has often created whizbang solutions in search of a problem, we are dedicated to bringing convenience and enhancements to proven training solutions. All our e-tools comply with rigorous functionality standards. The most appropriate technology wrapped around essential content yields the perfect solution for today's on-the-go trainers and human resource professionals.

Pfeiffer
www.pfeiffer.com

Essential resources for training and HR professionals

Employee Opinion Questionnaires

20 Ready-to-Use
Surveys That Work

Paul M. Connolly, Ph.D.
Kathleen Groll Connolly

Pfeiffer
A Wiley Imprint
www.pfeiffer.com

Copyright © 2005 by John Wiley & Sons, Inc.

Published by Pfeiffer
An Imprint of Wiley.
989 Market Street, San Francisco, CA 94103-1741   www.pfeiffer.com

For additional copies/bulk purchases of this book in the U.S. please contact 800-274-4434.

Pfeiffer books and products are available through most bookstores. To contact Pfeiffer directly call our Customer Care Department within the U.S. at 800-274-4434, outside the U.S. at 317-572-3985, fax 317-572-4002, or visit www.pfeiffer.com.

Pfeiffer also publishes its books in a variety of electronic formats. Some content that appears in print may not be available in electronic books.

ISBN: 0-7879-7349-1

Library of Congress Cataloging-in-Publication Data
Connolly, Paul M.
   Employee opinion questionnaires: 20 ready-to-use surveys that work/
Paul M. Connolly, Kathleen Groll Connolly.
      p. cm.
   ISBN 0-7879-7349-1
   1. Employee attitude surveys. I. Connolly, Kathleen Groll. II. Title.
   HF5549.5.A83C66   2004
   658.3'14—dc22
                                                      2004020733

Acquiring Editor: Martin Delahoussaye
Director of Development: Kathleen Dolan Davies
Developmental Editor: Susan Rachmeler
Production Editor: Rachel Anderson

Editor: Bev Miller
Manufacturing Supervisor: Bill Matherly
Editorial Assistant: Laura Reizman
Illustration: Lotus Art

Printed in the United States of America

Printing   10   9   8   7   6   5   4   3   2   1

Contents

CD-ROM Contents

Employee Opinion Questionnaires: 20 Ready-to-Use Surveys That Work

Questionnaire 1: Employee Opinion Survey on Employee Morale

Questionnaire 2: Employee Opinion Survey on Employee Benefits

Questionnaire 3: Employee Opinion Survey on Organizational Change

Questionnaire 4: Employee Opinion Survey on Employee Engagement

Questionnaire 5: Employee Opinion Survey on Communications

Questionnaire 6: Employee Opinion Survey on Compensation

Questionnaire 7: Employee Opinion Survey on Coworker Relations

Questionnaire 8: Employee Opinion Survey on Fairness and Diversity

Questionnaire 9: Employee Opinion Survey on the Individual Employee's Manager

Questionnaire 10: Employee Opinion Survey on Management

Questionnaire 11: Employee Opinion Survey on Job Satisfaction

Questionnaire 12: Employee Opinion Survey on Workplace Resources and Safety

Questionnaire 13: Employee Opinion Survey on Organizational Mission and Values

Questionnaire 14: Employee Opinion Survey on Innovation and Creativity

Questionnaire 15: Employee Opinion Survey on Quality Practices

Questionnaire 16: Employee Opinion Survey on Customer Care

Questionnaire 17: Employee Opinion Survey on Ethics

Questionnaire 18: New Employee Survey

Questionnaire 19: Exit Survey

Questionnaire 20: Training Effectiveness Survey

Exhibits

Exhibit 7.3: Sample Communications Survey Awareness
Letter for a Large Organization

Introduction

How to Get the Most from This Resource

EMPLOYEE MORALE and opinions don't stand still for the annual organizationwide survey. As a manager, neither can you. If you need to understand attitude changes quickly, short surveys on the topics of the day may be right for you.

Perhaps these are familiar employee comments:

"We can't get any cooperation from the other departments."

"We've got a real us-them outlook developing. I can't figure out why."

"I just can't get this group to work as a team."

Business outcomes depend on managing these situations in a matter of days or weeks, not months or years. If your work group is too big, if people need to be convinced of a real issue, or if the questions you need answers to are too sensitive to explore in a few informal conversations, the surveys in this book will help you get the information you need systematically, effectively, and quickly.

Questionnaire development is surprisingly time-consuming. Questionnaires may seem simple, but in reality, they are complex to write. We have seen organizations take two to four months to develop their own questionnaires, and much of that time is spent on internal negotiations among stakeholders. There can be disagreement around what to ask and how to ask it. Often, to keep the number of questions low, two, three, or more thoughts are included in a single question, hardly conducive to obtaining reliable answers. The wording and order are important, and good wording is not always obvious.

This book will help you get the answers you need more quickly than you would if you were were faced with developing a reliable questionnaire. They are designed for use in short, focused employee surveys where your goal is to obtain limited information. It is important to note here that we use the term *survey* in referring to the entire polling process. We use the term *questionnaire* in referring to the actual polling instrument. To get the most from this book, we recommend four steps.

First, decide if a short, focused questionnaire is right for your situation. In Chapter One, we define employee surveys and then discuss the role of these surveys. We also discuss the value of standard questionnaires, such as the ones in this book, as well as the role of custom-developed questionnaires.

Second, use Chapter Two to find out what other employers are asking and what their employees are telling them. In Chapter Two, we present the ten questions our clients have asked most often, the ten questions that tend to get the least favorable response, and the ten questions that get the most favorable response. We supply a complete set of norms for the thirty items, along with a description of the Employee Feedback Database, a collection of employee opinion norms for topics of key interest to employers. These norms are based on sixty thousand employee responses obtained from 139 surveys we have performed since 1999 for forty employers. The core questions are consolidated into a thirty-item general morale questionnaire, which you can use.

Third, determine which topical questionnaire is correct for your situation. In Chapter Three, we outline 100 organizational situations and suggest questionnaires to address them. Find the problems you're trying to address, and review the possible questionnaires.

Fourth, after selecting one or more surveys, read Chapters Seven through Ten for the insider tips that can make a difference during implementation and follow-up. We cover planning, questionnaire customization, report preparation, data interpretation, feedback meetings, and action planning. If you are new to the topic of employee opinion surveys, these chapters will be especially helpful.

Follow these steps and you can go forward confidently and speedily to gather the information you need to make improvements sooner rather than later.

Chapter 1

What Is a Quick Questionnaire? And When Should You Use One?

WHAT'S IN THIS CHAPTER?

- Short Surveys in Organizational Measurement
- Customized Questionnaires versus Standard Questionnaires
- Limitations of Surveys Performed by In-House Staff
- How to Find a Questionnaire
- Next Steps After Selecting a Survey

Short Surveys in Organizational Measurement

Think for a minute of organizational measurement as photography. Employee surveys are like group photos, both formal and informal. The full-length, periodic, organizationwide employee survey is a formal group photo. It requires lots of effort from many people in order to succeed. A full-length employee survey usually contains fifty to one hundred questionnaire statements, called *items*.

A short, focused survey, by contrast, is a snapshot. It is a brief, occasional poll that is usually carried out in response to a specific need. Snapshots aren't designed to tell the whole story. They excel at capturing slices of organizational life. This book addresses the snapshot. Most of the questionnaires in this book are ten to twenty items long. Because they are short and ready for use, we call them *quick questionnaires*. Exhibit 1.1 shows where they fit among the types of employee surveys.

EXHIBIT 1.1

Questionnaires Presented in This Book

	Full-Length Surveys	**Short, Focused Surveys**
Customized questionnaires	Often developed in conjunction with a survey professional	See Chapter Eight
Standard questionnaires	Developed through multiple repetitions until no further revisions are required	Quick questionnaires

---

In our consulting practice, we hear requests for all types of measurement. Organizations often ask for portraits—psychological or behavioral assessments—intended to help individuals increase their success on the job. Yet these portraits tell little about the context in which the individuals work. An organization's human resource department might request 360-degree feedback, for instance, to develop managers' skills. But the environment in which they practice their skills will either support or inhibit their individual skills and efforts. For this reason, the group opinion poll is sometimes the best place to start.

Short, focused surveys can address all of the topics that longer surveys address, just not as many of them at once. They can help with the small midcourse corrections that, uncorrected, might lead the organization far astray of its destination. But the quick questionnaires in this book are not just short versions of full-length employee survey questionnaires. The two types of questionnaires have different uses. Exhibit 1.2 compares and contrasts the two.

Chapter Two discusses the broad questions that many organizations ask and supplies a template for a general morale survey. Chapter Three supplies a subject index to the questionnaires in later chapters. It shows how to identify which questionnaires in this book can be used to address the issues. Before selecting a questionnaire, though, there are two topics to consider: the value of customized versus standard surveys, such as those presented in this book, and in-house versus third-party survey administration.

Customized Questionnaires versus Standard Questionnaires

In acquiring this book, you have added some standard questionnaires to your toolbox. Standard questionnaires are written for use "as is" in a broad assortment of situations. They should contain items that have been used in

EXHIBIT 1.2

Comparison of a Full-Length Employee Survey with a Short, Focused Survey

Your Employee Survey Goals	Use a Full-Length Employee Survey	Use a Short, Focused Questionnaire
Establish a long-term survey program.	✓	
Make a broad assessment of organizational culture.	✓	
Determine if specific aspects of culture are changing.		✓
Determine if there's movement in one or two baseline opinions.		✓
Gather reactions to sudden or major changes in the work environment.		✓
Measure opinions on a broad set of topics.	✓	
Measure opinions on a limited and specific topic.		✓
Measure opinions organizationwide, across all work units.	✓	
Measure opinions in smaller units.		✓
Create a benchmark before a major change initiative.	✓	
Determine how a major change initiative is perceived.		✓
Create an inventory of training needs.	✓	
Determine if training needs are being met by training efforts.		✓
Determine if management is communicating effectively overall.	✓	
Determine if management is communicating effectively within specific units or on specific issues.		✓
Follow up to a longer or routinely scheduled survey.		✓

multiple situations and refined through usage. Customized questionnaires are written for a specific situation. They employ situation-specific language and concepts and are designed for one-time use or repeated use within a single organization. Each type of questionnaire presents advantages and disadvantages.

Strengths of Customized Questionnaires

If an organization has a specific mission statement, a vision, and a set of values, it has probably developed its own wording to describe these concepts. It also may have developed core competency statements for its jobs, which are the behaviors and skills that support the stated mission.

A customized questionnaire can target specific issues or competencies and use language familiar to members of the organization. It can incorporate terms common to that organization, such as *colleagues, associates,* or *coworkers.* Customization can give the look and feel of an insider's writing. Thus, the survey and reports are better positioned to gain support from key stakeholders. Customization is also helpful when people in many locations will be surveyed, because the questionnaire may contain location-specific questions and reports.

But a big question is this: *How easy is it to create your own customized questionnaire?* On the surface, questionnaire creation may appear easy. But in our experience, each usable questionnaire item takes about thirty to forty-five minutes to create—and that comes after what can be difficult negotiation over selection of topics. If the instrument is standard length, it will contain fifty to one hundred items. Therefore, the development time is significant. Moreover, this work usually involves several people and several reviews. Surveys, in other words, are often more difficult to create than they appear.

In addition, questions must be carefully tested. Wording must be clear to all audiences, or their responses may obscure the meaning of the data, hardly what anyone wants.

Comparative results are also an issue. On first administration, a new survey item will yield results that have little or no basis for comparison. And sometimes the results contain no message at all. Consider the distribution of results from the following question:

The management training offered over the past year has been effective.

Totally disagree	*35 percent*
Somewhat disagree	*5 percent*
Neutral	*30 percent*
Somewhat agree	*5 percent*
Strongly agree	*25 percent*

How should you interpret this result? This particular response distribution is *trimodal* (meaning that it has three relatively equal response groups), and so the item is a poor candidate for further use. We know only that people's viewpoints range from poor to excellent in relatively equal numbers. It's hard to get a message from the data—except the message that additional research may be needed.

When to Use a Custom Questionnaire

A university adopted five core values that were intended to drive its business practices: Pursuit of Knowledge, Respect for Individuals, Academic Stewardship, Service to the Community, and Excellence. The principles were intended to inform not only service delivery to students but also relations with other stakeholders, such as suppliers and employees. There was disagreement among the administration over whether these values could or should apply to employees. After prolonged discussion, they decided the values must apply in all cases. Otherwise, they were simply customer services practices, not core values.

Sometimes the discussion about the implications was heated. For instance, the university had a community outreach program for single parents in which it provided short-term day care so that they could attend classes. But employees could not use the short-term day care to attend to their own needs or complete their own degrees. In fact, some employees in hourly positions were disciplined if they were as little as three minutes late. In other words, clients were treated in alignment with the stated value, but employees were treated another way.

The institution decided to do an employee survey to measure the beliefs about the core values and gauge their acceptance. It created customized items to reflect the values, but also selected standard ques-tions that fit the value definitions. Some customized values statements included these:

> Respect for individuals: "I feel I am treated with respect by my coworkers."
>
> Service to the community: "I feel this university is involved in and committed to improving life in our geographic region."
>
> Excellence: "Employees in my department are willing to put in as much effort as is necessary to get the job done to the best of our ability."

When the administrators saw the core values translated into employee questionnaire items, they got their first eye-opener. They didn't need to do a survey to realize there were instances of mixed messages. Ultimately, they did the survey, and the results supported their suspicions. They recognized that their stated values looked like window dressing. They had to improve alignment and took several quick steps to reduce the gaps.

A custom questionnaire was best in this situation because the organization had well-defined core values and beliefs. It also detected specific gaps between words and actions in the workplace. The university aimed for alignment on specific issues. Within a year, another administration of the survey showed that alignment had indeed improved.

In summary, the quick questionnaires in this book are a time-saving resource, but sometimes customized questionnaires are called for. If you need a few customized questions, see Chapter Eight. If you need an entire customized questionnaire, survey professionals are well equipped to help.

Value of Standard Questionnaires

Survey outcome has as much to do with productive discussion of work and reward issues as it does with information gathering. The use of surveys gives an organization the potential to make progress and exchange honest feedback. It removes the dynamics of face-to-face conversation and avoidance of subjects that might lead to conflict.

The survey questionnaires themselves, whether standard or custom, are vehicles, not ends in themselves. The real leverage of an employee survey is in the activity of the people who carry it out. Thus, a well-crafted general questionnaire that follows the rules of good item writing can do an excellent job.

A standard questionnaire should, by definition, have several administrations before it becomes "standard." With repeated use, the items can be refined and improved so they are well understood by most employees and are proven to gather valuable information.

Norms are based on the repetitive use of survey items. Each time a question is asked, the response data can be added to the averages behind that question. If your organization's responses differ from the average, you can investigate the reasons. Such differences can lead to more interesting questions or provide assurance that you are doing better than other organizations or than your own organization under a prior administration.

A Short, Focused Survey Did the Job

A law firm with sixty employees was experiencing unwanted turnover. The human resource manager suspected the problem but needed data to support his assumptions. Two of the partners, both highly skilled attorneys, were unskilled as managers and were driving talent out of the firm. Despite repeated suggestions for training, the partners felt they were too busy and the firm's revenues too dependent on their case activity to take time away for management development. The senior partners never witnessed these lawyer-managers' unskilled handling of employees; they saw only that the two were very skilled lawyers. In frustration, the human resources manager turned to a twenty-one-item survey on management practices, similar to the Employee Opinion Survey on the Individual Employee's Manager in Chapter Four. When results were reported, the two unskilled partners' numbers told the story. Among the most telling items were these:

"My manager gives me adequate feedback on the work I do."	48 percent unfavorable
"My manager is fair in dealing with people."	45 percent unfavorable
"My manager sets clear goals and objectives."	41 percent unfavorable

Each item received more than 40 percent disagreement, with the item on feedback leading the pack. The conclusions were inescapable, and the senior partners finally understood the implications. The two unskilled managers were signed up to attend training. One of the attorneys soon relinquished management responsibilities and returned to individual contributor status. The other went on to get additional management development. Within six months, turnover dropped significantly.

Standard Surveys and Comparative Data

While you're planning your reports, consider whether you wish to develop norms. In most employee survey work, norms are represented by the mean, median, and standard deviation of responses to a question. They describe how employees at other companies who have taken the same survey answered the same or similar question. They help compare your organization's performance to other organizations on key questions and show how you differ from the average (Exhibit 1.3). See the questionnaire items in Chapter Two, which are provided with norms from our database of more than sixty thousand survey responses.

EXHIBIT 1.3

General Norm versus Results for Your Organization

Considering everything, I am satisfied working for this organization at the present time.

	Strongly Disagree, Disagree	Neutral	Strongly Agree, Agree	Mean Score on a Five-Point Scale
General industry	17.6%	18.5%	63.9%	3.62 ($N = 60,205$)
Your organization	23.8	24.4	51.8	3.36 ($N = 888$)

Source: *Performance Programs, Inc., Employee Feedback Database, 2004.*

Without the normative information, you would not know that you are weaker than a sample of companies in the general employment market. Norms illustrate the similarity of your weak or strong areas to other employers. We supply norms for thirty items in this book. For instance, in Chapter Two, the questions with the least favorable responses show where many organizations score poorly. Communications and compensation, for instance, are weighted toward the unfavorable side by most everyone. Your organization may need to work on these areas, but the general norms may show that everyone else does too.

Norms help prioritize change efforts, but they can also have false allure. They may feed curiosity or fuel a competitive streak. Remember that your organization's capacity to improve is your chief concern. Work on your areas of relative vulnerability. If you plan, you can develop your own norms after one or two repetitions of a questionnaire. Internal norms are valuable and recommended because they help monitor the effectiveness of the organization's responses to its actual challenges.

Limitations of Surveys Performed by In-House Staff

The questionnaires in this book will help you conduct your own surveys. Nevertheless, you should consider the following points before choosing to conduct the survey using in-house personnel. The issues raised here are true whether you use the questionnaires in this book or develop your own.

Perception of Safety

Using an outside research firm can increase respondents' confidence in the promise of anonymity. It increases the employee's perception that any unflattering rating he or she gives will remain anonymous. This confidence in anonymity boosts response rates and increases the likelihood that employees will give candid information.

Process Consulting

A professional survey provider brings expertise to the survey process itself. The vendor can review the survey plan, communications, and feedback approach. He or she should know how to avoid errors such as ineffective presurvey communications, unclear survey instructions, unclear deadlines, and problems with survey or report formats. It has been our observation that the administrative process is where many in-house surveys fail. We have often been asked to step in when a survey was faltering.

Norms

Norms provide outside comparison for the questionnaire items on the survey. Survey professionals can often determine whether your results are typical for your type and size of business.

Report Formatting and Production

It is best to design and format employee survey reports before the questionnaire is finished, an issue that most in-house survey producers don't think about ahead of time. If for this reason alone, you might want to use an experienced survey provider or buy a software product that has templates specifically designed for employee surveys. Reports, after all, are what you want from the project. They are the beginning of the all-important feedback stage. The number and variety of reports, however, can become daunting. We've produced as many as four hundred different reports for a single employee survey. Acceptable reports can be produced by many common software packages.

How to Find a Questionnaire

Chapter Three provides a list of one hundred symptoms of organizational difficulty and suggests surveys to address them. If you wish to go directly to the questionnaires, they are organized in four ways: top employee survey questions (Chapter Two), issue-focused surveys (Chapter Four), mission-focused surveys (Chapter Five), and event-related surveys (Chapter Six).

As you begin to read and use the surveys themselves, you may see some blurring of the distinctions among them. The issue-focused questionnaires speak to traditional problem areas, but also to an organization's aims and sometimes could as easily be classified as mission focused. The mission-focused questionnaires speak to organizational ideals—but since no organization ever achieves all of its goals, they could also be viewed as issue focused. We offer some rules for selecting among the categories along with brief descriptions.

Top Employee Survey Questions

The thirty-item collection in Chapter Two is based on research in our questionnaire database. It contains the ten questions our clients have asked most often, the ten questions that tend to have the most negative response, and the ten that have the most positive response. You may wish to use the items as a survey or simply refer to them as a resource when developing your own survey. Each item in this section is accompanied by norms from our database.

If this is your first survey and you aren't sure of the issues, you might use this as an exploratory survey. Since norms accompany these items, you'll have a basis for comparing your results with results of others who have taken the surveys. However, remember that this questionnaire was extrapolated from a collection of eighty-five questions and is not focused on any particular topic.

Issue-Focused Surveys

Eleven issue-focused questionnaires cover common topics that trouble many organizations: communications, one's own manager, management in general, job satisfaction, organizational change, coworker relations, fairness and diversity, employee engagement, workplace resources and safety, compensation, and benefits. These are provided in Chapter Four.

Mission-Focused Surveys

Five questionnaires are designed to probe employee understanding of the organization's vision or values or acceptance of its strategy. They address the topics of organizational mission and values, innovation and creativity, quality practices, customer care, and ethics. They measure whether leadership messages make the right impression. For instance, what is the readiness for hearing and accepting messages surrounding ethics? Customer care? Safety? Quality? These questionnaires are in Chapter Five.

Event-Related Surveys

Three questionnaires are designed for specific points in time: new hire, exit, and posttraining. These are provided as examples, but may require customization depending on your situation. We provide more detail in Chapter Six.

Next Steps After Selecting a Survey

After selecting one or more surveys, read Chapters Seven through Ten for the insider tips that can help your survey be successful. If you are inexperienced with surveys, these chapters will be especially helpful. For an even more thorough look or for a complete guide to creating an entire survey process, you may want to get a copy of our books: *Employee Surveys: Practical and Proven Methods, Samples, Examples* and its companion volume *The Employee Survey Question Guidebook.**

•   •   •

An employee survey creates an opportunity to communicate about the health of an organization. Much of its value is in the process and the conversations that ensue. If you follow the steps set out in this book, you will be on your way to getting better information, and better discussion, about your organization.

---

* Connolly, P. M., and Connolly, K. G. *Employee Surveys: Practical and Proven Methods, Samples, Examples,* and its companion volume, *The Employee Survey Question Guidebook.* Old Saybrook, Conn.: Performance Programs, 2003.

Chapter 2

Top Employee Survey Questions

WHAT'S IN THIS CHAPTER?

- Employee Opinion Norms
- Ten Frequently Asked Employee Survey Questions
- Ten Questions with the Least Favorable Response
- Ten Questions with the Most Favorable Response
- Questionnaire 1: Employee Opinion Survey on Employee Morale

PERHAPS YOU'VE wondered what other organizations ask their employees and what their employees tell them. This chapter provides some insight into these questions.

We have surveyed more than five hundred organizations around the world, ranging in size from fifty employees to some of the largest employers in the world. They include commercial enterprises, schools, government organizations, and nonprofits.

As a result, we've developed questionnaires on many topics and have written hundreds of questions. We found a core group of eighty-five questionnaire items repeated in the majority of employee surveys out of a collection of more than 650 items we have used since 1987. Beginning in 1999, we changed the way we stored data so that we could study how employees respond to the core questions. The new method allowed us to develop the Employee Feedback Database, a collection of norms for the eighty-five core questions.

Employee Opinion Norms

Items in the Employee Feedback Database have been administered to as many as 60,000 people on 140 survey administrations. The forty organizations represented here are from both commercial and noncommercial industry classifications. About 20 percent of the response data is from multinational locations of U.S. corporations. As a result, the data represent what thousands of employees told their employers on surveys. They do not represent the outcome of a scientifically controlled study, nevertheless, they provide a basis for comparison with other employers who conducted research similar to yours with their employees.

Consider the following example from items in the database with the most negative responses:

I feel secure about my continued employment at this organization.

Strongly Disagree or Disagree	*36.6 percent*
Neutral	*21.9 percent*
Agree or Strongly Agree	*41.5 percent*

Thirty-seven percent disagreement would be considered a critically high level of dissatisfaction on a survey. If you used the same question, this response distribution could be used as a basis of comparison.

This chapter provides thirty of those core questions. It also provides the employee responses recorded by our organization since 1999. The items were selected based on the following analysis:

- Ten frequently asked questions

- Ten questions with the least favorable responses

- Ten questions with the most favorable responses

We present these data as an interesting look at what actual organizations ask and how their employees respond. The data may supply the comparison you need to feel confident in results from your own surveys. This is not presented as a scientifically designed study or as a standalone survey. It is based on a *convenience* sample, that is, a sample based on the data available to a researcher, in contrast to a scientifically designed sample, in which the researcher defines the data required before acquiring that information. You'll find the questions noteworthy for how often they're used, as well as for the answers they receive. They give a good idea of the issues that concern many employers—or that should concern them. Some of the question sets might not fit your survey needs, but they nevertheless are good points of reference.

In the next three sections, the questions and the associated data are presented. Each group of questions is described with the following five categories of data:

- Number of valid responses in the database (N). We selected only items that had at least five thousand responses.

- Number of surveys on which we recorded the question. We selected only items that had been asked on at least ten surveys.

- The mean or average response.

- The standard deviation of all responses.

- The percentage of unfavorable, neutral, and favorable responses. Although respondents could answer with five choices, ranging from Strongly Disagree to Strongly Agree, we have summarized them here under three general categories: Disagree, Neutral, and Agree. This is a common format for employee survey work.

Some questions have more than sixty thousand responses and were used in as many as 139 surveys. Other items have had considerably less use. Yet each has enough data to impart an approximation of viewpoints held by people in organizations. The questionnaire items were selected as we collaborated with each employer to meet its information needs.

The data are current as of April 2004. Our organization updates the Employee Feedback Database routinely. (To learn more, visit www. performanceprograms.com or call 1–800–565–4223.)

Ten Frequently Asked Employee Survey Questions

Some questions are asked of all or nearly all the respondents in the Employee Feedback Database. They are presented in Exhibit 2.1. The topics on this list include overall satisfaction:

Considering everything, I am satisfied working for this organization at the present time.

I see myself working for this organization three years from now.

Role clarity is also among the frequently asked questions:

I am clear about what I need to do and how my job performance will be evaluated.

My manager sets clear goals and objectives.

Training and support are on the list:

I receive the training I need to do my job.

I have the resources I need to do my job.

My manager takes a supportive role in my professional growth and development.

EXHIBIT 2.1

Ten Frequently Asked Employee Survey Questions

Rank	Questionnaire Statement (numbers in parentheses represent the question number in the norm database)	Number of Surveys Using the Question	Respondents Who Have Answered the Question	Mean	Standard Deviation	Unfavorable (%)	Neutral (%)	Favorable (%)
1	Considering everything, I am satisfied working for this organization at the present time. (1)	139	60,205	3.62	1.095	17.6	18.5	63.9
2	I receive the training I need to do my job. (25)	136	57,658	3.35	1.145	23.7	24.6	51.8
3	Employees are encouraged to offer their opinions and ideas. (41)	134	36,040	3.33	1.173	24.2	25.1	50.8
4	I am clear about what I need to do and how my job performance will be evaluated. (27)	134	54,930	3.69	1.065	15.1	18.1	66.9
5	I have the resources I need to do my job. (24)	134	55,981	3.45	1.084	20.3	23.1	56.6
6	I see myself working for this organization three years from now. (4)	131	51,331	3.71	1.169	15.7	21.2	63.1
7	People are encouraged to try new ways of doing things. (39)	130	52,483	3.49	1.073	18.1	25.9	56.0
8	My manager sets clear goals and objectives. (62)	128	40,876	3.68	1.017	13.4	20.7	65.9
9	My manager takes a supportive role in my professional growth and development. (61)	128	53,810	3.38	1.221	24.2	23.5	52.4
10	There is a strong feeling of team spirit and cooperation in this organization. (42)	128	43,574	3.59	1.210	19.7	16.4	63.9

Note: The numbers in parentheses refer to the item's position in our database. We include them here to facilitate inquiries about the items.

Source: Employee Feedback Database of Performance Programs, Old Saybrook, Conn.

Participation is covered by two questions:

Employees are encouraged to offer their opinions and ideas.

People are encouraged to try new ways of doing things.

Finally, team spirit is addressed by one item:

There is a strong feeling of team spirit and cooperation in this organization.

Noticeably missing from this list are communications, management, commitment, and compensation. All of these missing topics appear in the least favorable and most favorable lists. Perhaps the ten questions employers most like to ask are not the ones they need to ask.

Ten Questions with the Least Favorable Response

Some questions tend to get a high level of unfavorable response, no matter which organizations ask the question. Exhibit 2.2 presents ten that recorded the least favorable responses out of the eighty-five questions we track. For instance, communications is represented three times on this list of unfavorable items:

Overall, information in this organization is communicated well.

This organization listens to the ideas/opinions that employees contribute.

I am kept up-to-date on any organizational changes in policy or practice.

Apparently, there is a gap between employees' need for information and organizations' ability to provide it. In fact, one might wonder why the negativity isn't even greater. After all, a 31 percent negative rating for the first item, communications, is not a majority. The problem is that each unhappy employee interacts with many others on any given day, and their opinions can cloud the atmosphere. Our rule of thumb is that when dissatisfaction reaches 20 percent, it has probably reached a level where it should be carefully monitored. This is especially true if "neutral" opinions make up a large percentage, because they could swing to the negative side.

Compensation and benefits, both fairly predictable members of this list, have one question each:

This organization pays well compared to other organizations.

I am satisfied with the benefits package this organization offers.

Also significant on the negative list are the questions about future career development. Job security and view of the future also get low marks:

I feel secure about my continued employment at this organization.

I believe my career aspirations can be achieved at this organization.

EXHIBIT 2.2

Ten Least Favorable Employee Survey Questions

Rank	Questionnaire Statement (numbers in parentheses represent the question number in the norm database)	Number of Surveys Using the Question	Respondents Who Have Answered the Question	Mean	Standard Deviation	Unfavorable (%)	Neutral (%)	Favorable (%)
1	This organization pays well compared to other organizations. (69)	109	53,283	2.94	1.22	37.0	29.5	33.5
2	I feel secure about my continued employment at this organization. (52)	32	9,984	3.02	1.239	36.6	21.9	41.5
3	Overall, information in this organization is communicated well. (9)	30	5,281	3.08	1.104	31.3	28.3	40.4
4	I am satisfied with the benefits package this organization offers. (70)	10	9,718	3.08	1.208	34.1	24.1	41.8
5	Management is supportive of its employees. (76)	14	8,047	3.1	1.315	36.9	17.9	45.3
6	I believe my career aspirations can be achieved at this organization. (54)	53	49,478	3.14	1.183	30.6	27	42.4
7	I feel recognized for the contribution I make to this organization. (73)	104	49,438	3.15	1.229	31.3	24.3	44.4
8	This organization listens to the ideas/opinions that employees contribute. (80)	107	38,268	3.17	1.206	29.5	27.4	43.2
9	I am kept up-to-date on any organizational changes in policy or practice. (34)	114	18,296	3.24	1.189	26.9	24.4	48.7
10	I get the cooperation I need from those outside my department. (46)	44	32,810	3.24	1.027	23.8	29.9	46.3

Note: The numbers in parentheses refer to the item's position in our database. We include them here to facilitate inquiries about the items.

Source: Employee Feedback Database of Performance Programs, Old Saybrook, Conn.

Beliefs about their own future can motivate or discourage employees. The fact that two iterations of this question appear on the negative list should inspire you to include some career-oriented questions in your survey work.

We could make a similar observation about the recognition question that appears here:

I feel recognized for the contribution I make to this organization.

One interdepartmental coworker item got poor ratings, in contrast to the high ratings given to intradepartmental questions in the "most favorable" list in Exhibit 2.3:

I get the cooperation I need from those outside my department.

Finally, support from management was poorly rated:

Management is supportive of its employees.

This is a senior management question, not directly related to the respondent's immediate manager.

Ten Questions with the Most Favorable Response

The following questions are the ten that received the most favorable ratings out of eighty-five items we track. Items in the following areas received high ratings. Four of the most highly rated questions were about coworkers, three of them within the respondent's department:

The people I work with cooperate to get the job done.

The people I work with care a great deal about the quality of their work.

The people I work with help each other when there are problems.

People in this organization are willing to put in as much effort as necessary to get the job done.

Another three items spoke well of managers in this population:

My manager is accessible.

My manager backs me when necessary.

I would feel comfortable going to my manager with a concern.

Highly rated commitment questions include these three:

I am committed to seeing this organization succeed.

I am proud to be part of this organization.

I believe we can face the business challenges of the future.

•　　•　　•

EXHIBIT 2.3

Ten Most Favorable Employee Survey Questions

Rank	Questionnaire Statement (numbers in parentheses represent the question number in the norm database)	Number of Surveys Using the Question	Respondents Who Have Answered the Question	Mean	Standard Deviation	Unfavorable (%)	Neutral (%)	Favorable (%)
1	I am committed to seeing this organization succeed. (5)	46	27,736	4.06	1.041	9.1	14.6	76.3
2	I am positive we can face the business challenges of the future. (49)	46	29,058	4.01	.955	7.3	17.3	75.3
3	The people I work with cooperate to get the job done. (45)	38	13,424	3.96	.911	7.7	13.6	78.7
4	My manager is accessible. (63)	37	24,650	3.94	.989	9.7	13.5	77
5	My manager backs me when necessary. (64)	32	11,505	3.91	1.024	9.2	18.7	72.1
6	The people I work with care a great deal about the quality of their work. (6)	124	39,495	3.9	.949	8.8	16.5	74.7
7	I am proud to be part of this organization. (8)	43	26,763	3.9	1.024	9.7	19.9	70.4
8	I would feel comfortable going to my manager with a concern. (59)	44	14,366	3.86	1.115	13	14.7	72.3
9	The people I work with help each other when there are problems. (47)	48	24,760	3.85	.97	9.4	19.4	71
10	People are willing to put in as much effort as necessary to get the job done. (7)	35	8,012	3.82	.977	11.1	18.8	70.2

Note: The numbers in parentheses refer to the item's position in our database. We include them here to facilitate inquiries about the items.

Source: Employee Feedback Database of Performance Programs, Old Saybrook, Conn.

The three sets of questions in this chapter provide good insight into the types of questions employers are asking and how their employees are responding. Use these as a resource for your own questionnaire selections. Many of the items appear throughout the twenty questionnaires. You could use the norms here as a point of reference. The data are continuously updated as well. (For further information contact our organization at 1–800–565–4223 or surveys@performanceprograms.com.)

The "Normal" Distribution of Employee Survey Responses

You may notice that even the most negative responses in our database have a lot of positive, favorable responses. Perhaps they are more positive than you expected. High agreement with an item such as, "I am committed to seeing this organization succeed," may seem impossible given the recent focus of the news media on a "free agent" mentality among workers. And on the question of pay, 33.5 percent are in agreement with the statement that their organizations pay well compared to others.

Are people simply telling employers what they want to hear? Perhaps. In theory, the responses of survey populations larger than fifty individuals should approximate a normal bell-shaped curve. For instance, we typically use a five-point scale (1 is low and 5 is high) for employee survey work. Therefore, a normal distribution using this scale should produce a mean of 3.0 and a standard deviation of 0.8 to about 1.0. If we used a seven-point scale, the mean should be 3.5 with a standard deviation of about 1.0 to 1.2.

In practice, though, employee opinions in our database of sixty thousand responses do not follow a perfect normal curve. They are skewed toward the positive, with all items averaging 3.5 on a five-point scale in our experience. In other words, the average employee respondent seems to be biased toward a positive response. As groups grow larger, the more likely it is that their responses will average about 3.5. There could be a number of reasons for this, such as employees' believing that their employers want to see only positive responses. In some cases, employees may fear repercussions from negative answers. We don't know the exact reasons, but we know that the result has been consistent for years.

In this light, 76 percent agreement with the commitment statement on the "most favorable response" list doesn't look quite as high as it might at first. This is because the average score of all employee survey questions is higher than the predicted score.

We use this general phenomenon as a starting place for setting thresholds. There are some suggested thresholds and guidelines for interpreting survey responses in Chapter Nine.

You may wish to use these questions as presented to assess your own workforce. This question set represents a fairly broad mix of topics and would give a good picture of overall morale:

Questionnnaire 1. Employee Opinion Survey on Employee Morale

1. Considering everything, I am satisfied working for this organization at the present time.

2. I receive the training I need to do my job.

3. Employees are encouraged to offer their opinions and ideas.

4. I am clear about what I need to do and how my job performance will be evaluated.

5. I have the resources I need to do my job.

6. I see myself working for this organization three years from now.

7. People are encouraged to try new ways of doing things.

8. My manager sets clear goals and objectives.

9. My manager takes a supportive role in my professional growth and development.

10. There is a strong feeling of team spirit and cooperation in this organization.

11. This organization pays well compared to other organizations.

12. I feel secure about my continued employment at this organization.

13. Overall, information in this organization is communicated well.

14. I am satisfied with the benefits package this organization offers.

15. Management is supportive of its employees.

16. I believe my career aspirations can be achieved at this organization.

17. I feel recognized for the contribution I make to this organization.

18. This organization listens to the ideas/opinions that employees contribute.

19. I am kept up-to-date on any organizational changes in policy or practice.

20. I get the cooperation I need from those outside my department.

21. I am committed to seeing this organization succeed.

22. I am positive we can face the business challenges of the future.

23. The people I work with cooperate to get the job done.

24. My manager is accessible.

25. My manager backs me when necessary.

26. The people I work with care a great deal about the quality of their work.

27. I am proud to be part of this organization.

28. I would feel comfortable going to my manager with a concern.

29. The people I work with help each other when there are problems.

30. People are willing to put in as much effort as necessary to get the job done.

QUESTIONNAIRE 1

Employee Opinion Survey on Employee Morale

INSTRUCTIONS

This survey was designed to get feedback from you regarding your work experiences at our organization. The results of this survey will enable us to identify what we do well as an organization as well as identify areas that may need improvement. Your responses will be completely anonymous. Survey results will be reported in general terms and will not identify individuals. Please mark the number on the right that best represents your opinion, based on the scale below. Your feedback is greatly appreciated! Please be sure to use the following scale to define your response:

Strongly Disagree	Disagree	Neutral	Agree	Strongly Agree
1	2	3	4	5

1. Considering everything, I am satisfied working for this organization at the present time.   1 2 3 4 5
2. I receive the training I need to do my job.   1 2 3 4 5
3. Employees are encouraged to offer their opinions and ideas.   1 2 3 4 5
4. I am clear about what I need to do and how my job performance will be evaluated.   1 2 3 4 5
5. I have the resources I need to do my job.   1 2 3 4 5
6. I see myself working for this organization three years from now.   1 2 3 4 5
7. People are encouraged to try new ways of doing things.   1 2 3 4 5
8. My manager sets clear goals and objectives.   1 2 3 4 5
9. My manager takes a supportive role in my professional growth and development.   1 2 3 4 5
10. There is a strong feeling of team spirit and cooperation in this organization.   1 2 3 4 5
11. This organization pays well compared to other organizations.   1 2 3 4 5
12. I feel secure about my continued employment at this organization.   1 2 3 4 5
13. Overall, information in this organization is communicated well.   1 2 3 4 5
14. I am satisfied with the benefits package this organization offers.   1 2 3 4 5
15. Management is supportive of its employees.   1 2 3 4 5
16. I believe my career aspirations can be achieved at this organization.   1 2 3 4 5
17. I feel recognized for the contribution I make to this organization.   1 2 3 4 5
18. This organization listens to the ideas/opinions that employees contribute.   1 2 3 4 5
19. I am kept up-to-date on any organizational changes in policy or practice.   1 2 3 4 5
20. I get the cooperation I need from those outside my department.   1 2 3 4 5
21. I am committed to seeing this organization succeed.   1 2 3 4 5
22. I am positive we can face the business challenges of the future.   1 2 3 4 5
23. The people I work with cooperate to get the job done.   1 2 3 4 5
24. My manager is accessible.   1 2 3 4 5
25. My manager backs me when necessary.   1 2 3 4 5
26. The people I work with care a great deal about the quality of their work.   1 2 3 4 5
27. I am proud to be part of this organization.   1 2 3 4 5
28. I would feel comfortable going to my manager with a concern.   1 2 3 4 5
29. The people I work with help each other when there are problems.   1 2 3 4 5
30. People are willing to put in as much effort as necessary to get the job done.   1 2 3 4 5

QUESTIONNAIRE 1, Cont'd.

Employee Opinion Survey on Employee Morale

Please identify at least 2 or 3 things that we should be doing to improve as an organization:

Please identify at least 2 or 3 things that you like about working for this organization:

Thank you for your time and feedback!

Chapter 3

Selecting an Appropriate Survey

WHAT'S IN THIS CHAPTER?

- Survey Selection Grid

THIS CHAPTER SHOWS how to find the right questionnaire for the situations you want to address. The Survey Selection Grid in Exhibit 3.1 lists one hundred symptoms of organizational problems. Each symptom is accompanied by references to one or more surveys from the issue-focused, mission-focused, and event-related questionnaires that are examined in Chapters Four through Six.

The list of topics on the left (Column A) gives a general term, such as "Business Outlook" or "Career." These general terms are listed alphabetically. Column B lists problems that can arise under that category. Column C suggests questionnaires in this book that are related to these problems. This listing is not exhaustive; we recommend that you review each of the questionnaires as well. Symptoms are numbered in the order in which they first appear, but some numbers appear multiple times because they relate to more than one topic.

EXHIBIT 3.1

Survey Selection Grid

Column A: Topical Categories	Column B: 100 Organizational Symptoms or Problems	Column C: Related Questionnaires
Business outlook	1. Employees perceive the market for their products or services is declining	Management Innovation and Creativity Exit Survey Customer Care
	2. Employees view organization as ineffective in its marketplace	Management Organizational Change Customer Care Quality Practices
	3. Atmosphere of uncertainty	Organizational Mission and Values Management Employee Engagement Exit Survey
	4. Pessimism about the future	Employee Engagement
	5. Business decisions are widely questioned	Management Organizational Mission and Values Customer Care Exit Survey
Career	6. Employees feel blocked from internal job moves	Employee Engagement Exit Survey Individual Employee's Manager
	7. Employees feel blocked from career advancement by manager	Individual Employee's Manager Exit Survey
	8. Employees don't know what's required to get ahead within organization	Employee Engagement Individual Employee's Manager Organizational Mission and Values
	9. Jobs are perceived as dead-end; Employees feel lack of growth opportunities	Job Satisfaction Employee Engagement Innovation and Creativity Organizational Change Exit Survey
	10. Internal competition for advancement or prestige is intense	Coworker Relations Management

Note: The questionnaire titles in the third column are abbreviated. For example, the Employee Opinion Survey on Management is referenced here as "Management."

EXHIBIT 3.1

Survey Selection Grid, Cont'd.

Column A: Topical Categories	Column B: 100 Organizational Symptoms or Problems	Column C: Related Questionnaires
Change	11. Change efforts are proceeding poorly	Organizational Change
	12. The suggestion of change elicits resistance among some	Organizational Change Innovation and Creativity
	13. Employees comment that change is being stifled	Organizational Change Innovation and Creativity
Communication	14. Employees feel uninformed about their work	Communications Individual Employee's Manager Management Coworker Relations New Hire Workplace Resources and Safety
	15. Employees feel management doesn't listen	Communications Ethics Individual Employee's Manager Management
	16. Employees afraid to say what they think	Communications Ethics Individual Employee's Manager Management
	17. Employees confused about job requirements	Individual Employee's Manager Communications Job Satisfaction New Hire
	18. Information is perceived as partial and inadequate	Communications Individual Employee's Manager Management Organizational Mission and Values
	8. (Repeated) Employees don't know what's required to get ahead within organization	Individual Employee's Manager Employee Engagement
	19. Poor understanding of job description	Individual Employee's Manager Job Satisfaction New Hire
	20. Employees feel uninformed by top management	Organizational Mission and Values Management

EXHIBIT 3.1

Survey Selection Grid, Cont'd.

Column A: Topical Categories	Column B: 100 Organizational Symptoms or Problems	Column C: Related Questionnaires
	21. Employee roles in organizational goals unclear	Employee Engagement Management Job Satisfaction
	22. Policies are unclear	Communications New Hire
	23. Organization structure not clear	Individual Employee's Manager Management
	24. Employees feel "kept in the dark" by manager	Individual Employee's Manager Communications Exit Survey
	25. Plan is not clear to employees	Management Organizational Mission and Values
Compensation	26. Benefits are a frequent subject of negative discussion	Benefits
	27. Compensation levels are a frequent subject of negative discussion	Compensation
Conflict and lack of cooperation	28. Interdepartmental conflict is apparent	Coworker Relations Individual Employee's Manager
	29. Intradepartmental conflict is apparent	Coworker Relations Individual Employee's Manager
Customers	30. Lack of customer focus	Customer Care
	31. Out of touch with the marketplace	Management Innovation and Creativity Customer Care
	32. Employees disturbed by lack of quality in products or services	Ethics Customer Care Exit Survey
	33. Employees frustrated by customer demands and their ability to meet those demands	Quality Practices Customer Care
Diversity (also see Fairness)	34. Diversity—lack of comfort among definable groups with one another	Fairness and Diversity Individual Employee's Manager Coworker Relations Employee Engagement

EXHIBIT 3.1

Survey Selection Grid, Cont'd.

Column A: Topical Categories	Column B: 100 Organizational Symptoms or Problems	Column C: Related Questionnaires
Empowerment	35. Employees put in "just enough" effort to get by	Employee Engagement Job Satisfaction Management Individual Employee's Manager Compensation
	36. Lack of initiative and little independent thinking	Organizational Change Innovation and Creativity
	37. Lack of independent thinking and action	Innovation and Creativity
	38. Lack of caring about outcome of business efforts	Employee Engagement Management Organizational Mission and Values
Ethics	39. Uncertainty about freedom to discuss organization ethics	Ethics Management
	40. Suspiciousness of others in the organization, such as management or coworkers	Ethics Coworker Relations Management
Fairness (also see Diversity)	41. Complaints of unfair practices and attitudes	Fairness and Diversity Individual Employee's Manager Exit Survey
	42. Complaints about fairness in applying for and obtaining internal job opportunities	Fairness and Diversity Individual Employee's Manager Exit Survey
	43. Complaints that management is unfair	Management Fairness and Diversity Exit Survey
	44. Doubts about immediate manager's fairness	Individual Employee's Manager Fairness and Diversity
	45. Employees feel the performance evaluation process is unclear, unfair, or inadequate	Individual Employee's Manager Exit Survey
	46. Employees complain that resources and tools are unevenly or unfairly distributed	Job Satisfaction Workplace Resources and Safety Fairness and Diversity

EXHIBIT 3.1

Survey Selection Grid, Cont'd.

Column A: Topical Categories	Column B: 100 Organizational Symptoms or Problems	Column C: Related Questionnaires
Leadership	47. Employees lack confidence in management	Management Individual Employee's Manager
	48. Employees doubt manager's commitment	Individual Employee's Manager
	5. (Repeated) Business decisions are widely questioned	Management Organizational Mission and Values Customer Care
	49. Employees report they feel leaderless or that leaders are ineffective	Management Individual Employee's Manager
	50. Employees feel manager is ineffective, lacking confidence in manager's competence	Individual Employee's Manager
	51. Organization structure not clear	Management Communications
	52. Poor understanding of role in the organization	Individual Employee's Manager Job Satisfaction Exit Survey
Manager	53. Manager's department has high turnover	Employee Engagement Individual Employee's Manager Exit Survey
	54. Morale is poor in manager's department	Employee Engagement Employee Morale Individual Employee's Manager Exit Survey
Mission	55. Sense of mission is missing	Organizational Mission and Values Management
Morale	35. (Repeated) Employees put in "just enough" effort to get by	Employee Morale Employee Engagement Job Satisfaction Management Individual Employee's Manager
	56. Alienation from immediate manager, frustration with ability to influence own work outcomes	Employee Morale Individual Employee's Manager Exit Survey

EXHIBIT 3.1

Survey Selection Grid, Cont'd.

Column A: Topical Categories	Column B: 100 Organizational Symptoms or Problems	Column C: Related Questionnaires
	57. General dissatisfaction	Employee Morale Employee Engagement Exit Survey
	58. Employees feel alienated from top management	Employee Morale Management
	59. Employees lack motivation	Employee Morale Employee Engagement
	60. Employees feel unsupported by manager	Employee Morale Individual Employee's Manager
	61. Lack of caring about outcome of business efforts	Employee Morale Employee Engagement Organizational Mission and Values
	62. Job is perceived as boring	Employee Morale Job Satisfaction Exit Survey
	63. Employees feel their personal lives are overwhelmed by work	Employee Morale Employee Engagement Exit Survey
	64. Frustration with workload	Employee Morale Workplace Resources and Safety Employee Engagement Job Satisfaction Exit Survey Compensation
	65. Employees feel the physical workplace is unsafe	Employee Morale Workplace Resources and Safety Exit Survey
Participation	66. Alienation from management's decisions	Individual Employee's Manager Management
Performance	67. Goals and objectives are not emphasized in performance reviews	Individual Employee's Manager
	68. Employees feel the performance evaluation process is unclear, unfair, or inadequate	Individual Employee's Manager Exit Survey

EXHIBIT 3.1

Survey Selection Grid, Cont'd.

Column A: Topical Categories	Column B: 100 Organizational Symptoms or Problems	Column C: Related Questionnaires
	69. Low performance standards	Individual Employee's Manager Coworker Relations Quality Practices Customer Care
Planning	70. Employees confused about their roles in organizational goals	Management Organizational Mission and Values
	71. Overall plan is not apparent to employees	Organizational Mission and Values Management
Policies	72. Policies are unclear	Communications Organizational Mission and Values
Pride	73. Lack of pride in coworkers	Coworker Relations
	74. Lack of pride in the organization	Individual Employee's Manager Employee Engagement Exit Survey
	75. Lack of pride in products	Customer Care Quality Practices Exit Survey
Quality	76. Production quality not up to expectations or standards	Quality Practices Workplace Resources and Safety Coworker Relations Individual Employee's Manager Organizational Mission and Values
	77. Quality practices are sacrificed to meet production goals	Quality Practices Exit Survey
Recognition	78. Employees complain of a general lack of feedback in the organization	Individual Employee's Manager Communications
	79. Employees feel unrecognized by the organization	Individual Employee's Manager Management Job Satisfaction Exit Survey
Recruiting and Hiring	80. Lack of referrals by employees	New Employee Survey Employee Engagement

EXHIBIT 3.1

Survey Selection Grid, Cont'd.

Column A: Topical Categories	Column B: 100 Organizational Symptoms or Problems	Column C: Related Questionnaires
	81. Complaints about new employee orientation	New Employee Survey
	82. Complaints about the hiring process	New Employee Survey
	83. Instances where employees claim their jobs are not the same as described during the recruitment process	New Employee Survey Exit Survey
Resources	84. Employees complain of lack of tools to get the job done	Workplace Resources and Safety Job Satisfaction Exit Survey
	85. Employees feel that physical conditions are undermining their work	Workplace Resources and Safety Exit Survey
Team	86. Team spirit is missing	Coworker Relations
	87. Camaraderie is absent between departments	Coworker Relations
	88. Employees question the competence of their coworkers	Coworker Relations
	89. Camaraderie is absent among coworkers within departments	Coworker Relations
Training	90. Perceived lack of training opportunities	Workplace Resources and Safety Job Satisfaction Exit Survey
	91. Available training is perceived as inadequate or inappropriate	Training Effectiveness Job Satisfaction Exit Survey Workplace Resources and Safety
	92. Dissatisfied with training	Training Effectiveness Exit Survey
Trust	93. Mistrust of employer's intentions	Management Employee Engagement Ethics Individual Employee's Manager
	94. Fear of expressing opinions	Ethics Individual Employee's Manager Management

EXHIBIT 3.1

Survey Selection Grid, Cont'd.

Column A: Topical Categories	Column B: 100 Organizational Symptoms or Problems	Column C: Related Questionnaires
	95. Mistrustful atmosphere	Ethics Management Individual Employee's Manager Coworker Relations
Turnover	96. Good employees are leaving	Employee Engagement Compensation Individual Employee's Manager Innovation and Creativity Exit Survey
	97. Unwanted turnover among particular demographic groups (age, race, ethnicity, religion, sexual orientation, other)	Diversity and Fairness Individual Employee's Manager Exit Survey Coworker Relations
Values	98. Stated values are not perceived consistent with organization actions	Organizational Mission and Values Management
Work-life balance	99. Lost productivity due to family and personal demands	Employee Engagement Exit Survey
Workload	100. Complaints about overwork	Employee Engagement Job Satisfaction Individual Employee's Manager Exit Survey

Chapter 4

Surveys That Focus on Issues

WHAT'S IN THIS CHAPTER?

- Questionnaire 2. Employee Opinion Survey on Employee Benefits
- Questionnaire 3. Employee Opinion Survey on Organizational Change
- Questionnaire 4. Employee Opinion Survey on Employee Engagement
- Questionnaire 5. Employee Opinion Survey on Communications
- Questionnaire 6. Employee Opinion Survey on Compensation
- Questionnaire 7. Employee Opinion Survey on Coworker Relations
- Questionnaire 8. Employee Opinion Survey on Fairness and Diversity
- Questionnaire 9. Employee Opinion Survey on the Individual Employee's Manager
- Questionnaire 10. Employee Opinion Survey on Management
- Questionnaire 11. Employee Opinion Survey on Job Satisfaction
- Questionnaire 12. Employee Opinion Survey on Workplace Resources and Safety

THE ELEVEN SURVEYS described in this chapter can be used to diagnose common problem areas. Each survey has between ten and twenty-one items, making it possible for each one to cover two to four closely related topics. For each survey, we explain its primary focus, what to expect from it, when it is best used, and considerations to weigh in selecting it.

Benefits

Items in this category cover employee satisfaction with associated benefit programs.

When to Use

The Employee Opinion Survey on Employee Benefits can be administered routinely each year to detect the popularity and importance of various benefits.

Considerations

Demographic questions may reveal that some benefits vary in their popularity within departments or age groups. You might want to add some open-ended questions here to gauge interest in new benefit programs or vendors.

Questionnaire 2. Employee Opinion Survey on Employee Benefits

1. I am satisfied with the benefits package this organization offers.

2. My fringe benefits are competitive with those of other organizations.

3. My benefits meet the needs of my family.

4. The benefits program influenced my decision to work for this organization.

5. I would be willing to pay more for better benefits.

6. I am satisfied with the amount of information I receive on the benefits program.

7. I understand the features of my total benefits package.

8. I feel I can get benefits information easily if I need it.

9. (Please answer the following statement thinking of the benefit that is most important to you.) My most important benefit is meeting my needs at this time.

10. Please name the benefit most important to you at this time.

Organizational Change

The Employee Opinion Survey on Organizational Change will help to reveal employees' beliefs about the organization's ability to succeed with a change effort. It gauges perceived flexibility and perceived support for change. Low agreement with the statements in this survey shows a poor atmosphere for introducing change initiatives, such as new systems, re-organizations, new procedures, and other internal operating matters. The results should help you design communications and other programs to increase acceptance of change. By asking for demographic data, you may identify specific groups that may have difficulty with change.

When to Use

This survey will help both before and after a major change initiative. It also helps when change appears to be the source of trouble—for example, when change efforts are proceeding poorly, indicating resistance to change; employees feel lack of growth opportunities because of resistance to change; previous change efforts have not been successful; or senior management is not trusted.

Considerations

Views of flexibility and change are often different across levels. Therefore, it is important to add demographics to this survey by level and longevity with the organization, as well as by work unit. You must promise (and employees must believe) that you will not use this information to identify individual responses. If your organization is suffering from a lack of trust, this may be an issue. Consider keeping the demographics very general.

This is not the best survey for gauging receptivity to innovation in products and services or creative ways of interacting with the marketplace. These are best measured by the Employee Opinion Survey on Innovation and Creativity or the Employee Opinion Survey on Customer Care.

Questionnaire 3. Employee Opinion Survey on Organizational Change

1. Our values ensure that we change as our business environment changes.

2. I am committed to seeing change initiatives at my organization succeed.

3. Adequate communication to employees takes place prior to implementing new programs and/or systems.

4. Information about upcoming changes is delivered in a timely manner.

5. Change initiatives have helped our organization achieve its growth objectives.

6. This organization is making the changes necessary to compete effectively.

7. Our organization has a real interest in innovation.

8. Past change initiatives have had positive results.

9. The climate for change is very positive and supportive in my organization.

10. Constant improvement is valued by this organization.

Employee Engagement

The items in the Employee Opinion Survey on Employee Engagement cover elements that determine employees' overall engagement in their jobs and the organization: perceived value of the work, future career growth, optimism about the future, work-life balance, and interactions with management. These measurements suggest employees' commitment—their willingness to stay with the organization and to give full effort to the goals of the organization and the tasks of the individual job.

When to Use

This is a good basic barometer of employee engagement. It may be used on a routine basis to track opinions over time, but it is also suitable when a problem is detected. Evidence of pessimism and lack of pride in the organization are signs that commitment and engagement may be low. Some of the following symptoms may be evident:

- Uncertainty and pessimism about the organization's future

- Pessimism about one's own future with the organization; lack of perceived opportunity for career or salary growth

- People who put in just enough effort to "get by"

- Indifference, apathy

- Complaints of overwork

- Complaints that work is overwhelming personal life and that personal needs cannot be met; loss of productivity due to family demands that can't be handled

Considerations

Most of the items in this questionnaire are judgmental rather than observational. For instance, a question such as, "I am proud to be part of this organization," may give an idea of employees' feelings but not provide clear action items. These types of survey questions are often helpful in gauging whether further survey work or other investigation is needed. (See Chapter Eight on questionnaire development for a discussion of judgmental versus observational questions.)

Questionnaire 4. Employee Opinion Survey on Employee Engagement

1. Considering everything, I am satisfied working for this organization at the present time.

2. I am doing something I consider satisfying and worthwhile in my job.

3. My job is challenging and interesting.

4. I am proud to be part of this organization.

5. I am committed to seeing this organization succeed.

6. I see myself working for this organization three years from now.

7. I am confident we can face the business challenges of the future.

8. I am treated with dignity and respect.

9. I have the freedom I need to do my job.

10. I am involved with decisions that affect my work.

11. The work I do is very important to the success of my organization.

12. I am expected to produce significant but reasonable results.

13. I am satisfied with my opportunity for growth and development.

14. I believe my career aspirations can be achieved at this organization.

15. I am satisfied with the level of balance between my work and personal life.

16. I have the flexibility to arrange my work so that I can meet my business objectives and balance my family and personal needs.

Communications

The Employee Opinion Survey on Communications looks at four sources of information flow: the immediate manager, management in general, other work units, and immediate coworkers.

When to Use

Use this if you detect a breakdown in information flow among any of the four paths for communication. Symptoms include the following:

- Communication failures that are leading to quality or service problems

- Employees who report feeling uninformed

- Employees who feel that management doesn't listen to them or they can't say what they need to say

- Organization structure, job descriptions, or other key structural features that are unclear to employees

Considerations

Communications almost always seem deficient to employees. (See Chapter Two and the "least favorable" questions. Communications items receive some of the most unfavorable ratings in our database.) It is a lot like compensation, in that people have high expectations and may be difficult to please. The opportunity here may be to reduce the most negative responses rather than maximize positive responses.

Questionnaire 5. Employee Opinion Survey on Communications

1. My manager does a good job of keeping me informed about matters affecting me.

2. I receive the information I need about changes that affect my work.

3. Information is communicated in a timely manner.

4. Information is communicated openly and honestly in this organization.

5. This organization ensures policies and procedures are easy to understand.

6. Organizational goals and objectives are clearly explained to me.

7. I have enough information to do my job well.

8. Information about our organization's policies, practices, and procedures is easily available.

9. We are kept informed about important developments in different departments.

10. We are kept informed about important developments at different work locations.

11. This organization has adequate procedures for sharing information.

12. Coworkers share information willingly.

13. I would feel comfortable communicating openly with senior management if the need arose.

14. People communicate comfortably with one another in this organization regardless of position or level.

Compensation

The Employee Opinion Survey on Compensation focuses on salary and wages. Do employees feel they are paid fairly for the work they do compared with employees in other companies?

When to Use

This survey is helpful if unwanted turnover seems related to noncompetitive salaries or these symptoms appear:

- Attempts at manipulating the pay structure through overtime
- Attempts at manipulating the performance management system
- Unwanted turnover that is unrelated to satisfaction with one's manager

Considerations

All surveys raise expectations that something will change. Compensation is a topic that, by its nature, invites expectations that may be difficult to meet. If you ask questions about it, you must be certain you will be in a position to address at least some of the issues that come out. Be prepared for negativity too. This topic often brings out high levels of negative response.

It is important to combine the right demographic questions with this questionnaire. This is the only way to detect groups where dissatisfaction is greater than the average level for your organization.

Questionnaire 6. Employee Opinion Survey on Compensation

1. My total pay is adequate compared to other's in this organization.
2. Compensation practices at this organization are fair and reasonable.
3. Associates in my department are compensated (pay and benefits) fairly in relation to similar work elsewhere.
4. This organization pays me fairly for the work I do.
5. I understand how my compensation is determined.
6. I feel individuals are compensated appropriately as their responsibilities are increased.
7. People at this organization are rewarded according to their job performance.
8. This organization provides appropriate salaries considering duties and responsibilities.
9. My total earnings are fair considering my duties and responsibilities.
10. I would prefer an increase in my salary rather than improved or additional benefits.

Coworker Relations

The Employee Opinion Survey on Coworker Relations captures employees' experiences and feelings about the helpfulness and trust among coworkers. High scores on this survey are a good sign of sturdiness in the staff's relationships. When good relations are in place and hard times strike, the organization is more likely to be strong enough to weather them.

When to Use

This is a good diagnostic tool when there is evidence of poor team spirit, teams are unproductive, or there seems to be duplication of effort between functions or work units. Some symptoms include the following:

- Poor communication among coworkers
- Competition, mistrust, or conflict among coworkers
- Poor acceptance of people who are different in some way from most of the rest of the group (for example, race, religion, or gender)
- Poorly functioning teams and work output below expectations

Considerations

This survey does not fully address coworker competence, training, or other matters affecting productivity. These are addressed by the Employee Opinion Survey on the Individual Employee's Manager and the Employee Opinion Survey on Quality Practices.

Questionnaire 7. Employee Opinion Survey on Coworker Relations

1. People are willing to put in as much effort as necessary to get the job done.
2. People communicate comfortably with one another in this organization.
3. I get the cooperation I need from people outside my department.
4. The people I work with are friendly and helpful.
5. Employees in my organization generally trust one another and offer support.
6. The level of competitiveness within our organization is appropriate.
7. Employees in my department treat others with dignity and respect.
8. Employees in my department want to participate in important decisions that affect their work.
9. My coworkers have adequate training for the jobs they do.
10. People here seem committed to helping the organization succeed.
11. People participate willingly in efforts to improve performance in the department (quality, production, cost effectiveness, etc.).
12. People in my department understand that their actions have impact on the bottom line.
13. People in my department feel their time and efforts are used effectively.
14. People I work with help each other out when problems arise.

Fairness and Diversity

Diversity at one time meant fairness as it applied to protected classes. This is only one expression of fairness, however. The up-to-date iteration of this concept covers a wider perspective and range of issues. At its core, diversity issues relate to how comfortable employees are working with those they perceive as different from themselves. Differences might include the traditional protected classes, based on race, religion, and gender. It may also relate to sexual preference or bodily differences, such as weight or a visible disability.

When the atmosphere for fairness is poor, an employee subgroup may feel oppressed or persecuted. At the very least, they may feel ignored or marginal. In any case, the disruption created by attacking and defending groups can be substantial. It is a drag on productivity and morale.

This survey speaks to fairness to classes of employees and an atmosphere of dignity, respect, and fairness. It also can help determine whether differences in perspective are being used positively to enhance the organization.

When to Use

The Employee Opinion Survey on Fairness and Diversity is best used where issues of fairness have led to grievances or unwanted turnover. It will help gauge the organization's vulnerability to such issues. Some symptoms include the following:

- Complaints about unfairness of individuals
- Complaints about unfairness of policies and practices
- Inability to recruit or retain qualified minorities

Considerations

You will need to add suitable demographic questions to the survey, such as department, location, level, job classification, or other ways of measuring the organization. Because some managers may be anxious about the topic of this survey, they should be reassured they will see their results before upper management does. No department report should have fewer than five respondents. Individual managers should not be held responsible for survey results, only for their response to them.

Questionnaire 8. Employee Opinion Survey on Fairness and Diversity

1. Our organization treats employees fairly without regard to employment level.

2. All people, regardless of race, nationality, gender, age, or other individual characteristics, are given a fair opportunity to succeed in the organization.

3. There is a strong drive toward satisfying the needs of all employees in this organization.

4. Resources are allocated fairly.

5. I work in an environment where I feel comfortable being myself.

6. I am encouraged to treat others with dignity and respect.

7. The level of diversity at [organization name] is appropriate.

8. [Organization name] values the contributions of people with different work experience.

9. My work group makes good use of individual differences in style, approach, and skills.

10. My work group has a climate in which diverse perspectives are valued.

11. People in my work group communicate comfortably with others regardless of background.

12. Senior management demonstrates its support for diversity by its actions.

13. Our organization provides work assignments in a way that is fair to all employees.

14. This organization encourages a climate where diverse perspectives are valued.

The Individual Employee's Manager

People leave jobs to escape bad managers more often than for any other reason. The Employee Opinion Survey on the Individual Employee's Manager focuses on the employee's immediate manager. When there is neutral to strong disagreement with the statements in this survey, turnover is likely to be an issue. The survey provides a way to diagnose key elements of the manager-subordinate relationship, which are often at the heart of workplace problems.

When to Use

This survey has two distinct thrusts: the manager's interpersonal skills and the manager's organizational skills.

A manager's lack of interpersonal skills can lead to symptoms such as the following:

- Employees who feel blocked by the manager from career growth

- Intradepartmental conflict that is evident

- Issues with diversity and fairness

- Employees who are unclear about the method, timing, or effectiveness of performance evaluation and feel uninformed about expectations or the outcome of their work

- Employee apathy, alienation, or mistrustfulness

- Employees who report a lack of feedback and recognition

A manager's lack of organizational skills can lead to symptoms such as the following:

- Employee confusion over job definitions, goals, and objectives

- Conflict between managers and employees on a wide variety of topics

- People who feel unsupported by a manager and are unable or unwilling to support their manager

- Discussion and confusion over work tasks, due dates, and responsibilities

- People who express a lack of confidence in the manager's competence and effectiveness

- People who express a lack of confidence in the manager's commitment

- Performance and productivity that are below standards

- Complaints of overwork or inefficient use of employee time

Considerations

This survey must be carefully "sold" to managers of departments where it will be administered. Some managers will feel very threatened, especially because other important organizational areas won't be covered. ("It's not my fault," they might say. "It's senior management.") It will be very important to follow good survey implementation procedures. Be careful to avoid a "witch-hunt" atmosphere by emphasizing that the outcome will be shared first with the managers who are involved. Never report on any unit with fewer than five respondents. Always allow managers to see their departmental results before upper management sees them, and give them time to develop a response. This survey could be used instead of (or before) a behavioral 360-degree assessment.

Questionnaire 9. Employee Opinion Survey on the Individual Employee's Manager

1. My manager is fair in dealing with people.

2. My manager ensures that people who do a good job are recognized and appreciated.

3. My manager ensures that I am adequately informed about matters affecting me.

4. My manager gives me adequate feedback on the work I do.

5. My manager takes a supportive role in my professional growth and development.

6. My manager encourages me to do a good job.

7. My manager backs me when necessary.

8. I would feel comfortable going to my manager with a concern.

9. My manager helps me overcome barriers to getting the job done.

10. My manager communicates well with everyone in the department.

11. My manager involves me in decisions that affect my work.

12. My manager gives me the freedom I need to do my job.

13. My manager provides the resources I need to do my job.

14. My manager sets clear goals and objectives.

15. It is clear how my manager will evaluate my performance.

16. My manager sets work objectives that motivate people.

17. My manager uses good judgment in making decisions.

18. My manager effectively coordinates the work flow in our department.

19. My manager makes decisions promptly when needed.

20. My manager is in control of what is going on in our department.

21. My manager tries to assign work to maximize productivity.

Management

The Employee Opinion Survey on Management addresses respondents' feelings about management in general rather than their immediate managers.

When to Use

If employees are complaining they don't understand the direction that the entire organization is taking or that certain high-level actions make no sense to them, this survey may reveal the nature of senior management's credibility problem. Symptoms that suggest its use include the following:

- Pessimism about the future—the organization's opportunities as well as the individual's career growth opportunities

- Intense internal competition for advancement or prestige

- Poor credibility of the mission and values statements among employees
- A general sense among employees of feeling uninformed and unclear how to support organizational goals
- Lack of confidence in senior management and its business decisions
- Fairness and diversity issues
- Fear of communicating with senior management

Considerations

In our experience, the more distant an employee is from senior management in the organization structure, the more negative his or her beliefs about senior management are likely to be. This is somewhat predictable and should be considered in interpreting results.

Questionnaire 10. Employee Opinion Survey on Management

1. Top management is fair in dealing with people.
2. Management in my organization treats me with dignity and respect.
3. This organization values its employees.
4. Management will take action based on the results of this survey.
5. I have trust and confidence in the leadership of this organization.
6. There is genuine management concern for the problems employees face.
7. Management thinks creatively.
8. Management provides a clear picture of the long-term goals and direction of our organization.
9. Management has the ability to identify new business opportunities.
10. This organization is well managed.
11. Management acts consistently; they do as they say.
12. I would feel comfortable communicating openly with senior management if the need arose.

Job Satisfaction

How do employees feel about the work they do? The nature of work has enormous implications for productivity, morale, and other key features of organizational life. Topics such as personal sense of control over the work, sense of satisfaction, sense of accomplishment, and ability to see how the work fits in are covered in the Employee Opinion Survey on Job Satisfaction.

When to Use

Symptoms that indicate this survey is needed include the following:

- Tasks that are difficult to carry out by a number of people who hold (or held) the same job
- Low employee performance
- Employee complaints that their jobs are frustrating, boring, or dead-end
- Employees who don't see how the jobs fit with organizational goals
- Employee complaints of lack of resources or support to get a job done

Considerations

This survey will help diagnose problems in the recruitment and hiring process or possibly in job design or work processes. To devise solutions to those problems, you may need to use another survey or another problem-solving process altogether.

Questionnaire 11. Employee Opinion Survey on Job Satisfaction

1. My job makes good use of my skills and abilities.
2. I receive the training I need to do my job.
3. I am given opportunities to improve my skills in this organization.
4. My job is challenging and interesting.
5. I am doing something I consider satisfying and worthwhile in my job.
6. My job offers me the opportunity to gain work experience in challenging new areas.
7. I like my job at this organization.
8. I understand the link between what I do and the organization's objectives.
9. The work I do is very important to the success of my organization.
10. I am doing something I consider really worthwhile.
11. I really feel I accomplish something each day.
12. I have personal control over the way my work must be done.
13. I feel the amount of work required of me is about right.

Workplace Resources and Safety

Overall, the items on the Employee Opinion Survey on Workplace Resources and Safety measure the employee's perception of safety and adequacy of support systems in his or her working conditions. This survey detects several sources of workplace stress.

When to Use

This is a good way to diagnose problems leading to poor product quality or a high rate of safety incidents. Symptoms include the following:

- Complaints about lack of tools, resources, training, or support
- Frustration with high workloads that can compromise safety
- A sense among employees that the workplace is not secure or safe
- A sense among employees that physical working conditions are undermining the quality or safety of their work

Considerations

This survey helps diagnose imbalances, but it does not lead to deeper analysis of any single source of imbalance. Therefore, it is best used as a first-level diagnostic tool. Further analysis may require additional surveys or interviews.

Questionnaire 12. Employee Opinion Survey on Workplace Resources and Safety

1. I am clear about safety standards related to my work.
2. Safety standards are always followed.
3. I feel the amount of work required of me is about right.
4. My work environment enables me to be as productive as I can be.
5. I have enough information to do my job well.
6. The equipment provided is adequate.
7. I have the resources I need to do my job.
8. I receive the training I need to do my job.
9. I get the cooperation I need from those outside my department.
10. The physical security of my organization's facility is adequate.
11. Associates in my department make responsible decisions regarding the safety and welfare of themselves and others.
12. I know what procedure to follow in the event of an emergency.

• • •

The surveys in this chapter help measure the degree to which certain organizational problems are occurring in a particular workplace. The mission alignment surveys, discussed in Chapter Five, will help measure the degree to which employees perceive the organization's mission is effective in their daily working environment.

QUESTIONNAIRE 2

Employee Opinion Survey on Employee Benefits

INSTRUCTIONS

This survey was designed to get feedback from you regarding your employee benefits. The results of this survey will enable us to identify what we do well as an organization as well as identify areas that may need improvement. Your responses will be completely anonymous. Survey results will be reported in general terms and will not identify individuals. Please mark the number on the right that best represents your opinion, based on the scale below. Your feedback is greatly appreciated! Please be sure to use the following scale to define your response:

Strongly Disagree	Disagree	Neutral	Agree	Strongly Agree
1	2	3	4	5

1. I am satisfied with the benefits package this organization offers.   1 2 3 4 5
2. My fringe benefits are competitive with those of other organizations.   1 2 3 4 5
3. My benefits meet the needs of my family.   1 2 3 4 5
4. The benefits program influenced my decision to work for this organization.   1 2 3 4 5
5. I would be willing to pay more for better benefits.   1 2 3 4 5
6. I am satisfied with the amount of information I receive on the benefits program.   1 2 3 4 5
7. I understand the features of my total benefits package.   1 2 3 4 5
8. I feel I can get benefits information easily if I need it.   1 2 3 4 5
9. (Please answer the following statement thinking of the benefit that is most important to you.) My most important benefit is meeting my needs at this time.   1 2 3 4 5
10. Please name the benefit most important to you at this time:

QUESTIONNAIRE 2, Cont'd.

Employee Opinion Survey on Employee Benefits

11. Please identify anything we should be doing to improve benefits:

12. Please describe what benefits are meeting your needs:

Thank you for your time and feedback!

QUESTIONNAIRE 3

Employee Opinion Survey on Organizational Change

INSTRUCTIONS

This survey was designed to get feedback from you regarding your work experiences at our organization. The results of this survey will enable us to identify what we do well as an organization as well as identify areas that may need improvement. Your responses will be completely anonymous. Survey results will be reported in general terms and will not identify individuals. Please mark the number on the right that best represents your opinion, based on the scale below. Your feedback is greatly appreciated! Please be sure to use the following scale to define your response:

Strongly Disagree	Disagree	Neutral	Agree	Strongly Agree
1	2	3	4	5

1. Our values ensure that we change as our business environment changes. 1 2 3 4 5

2. I am committed to seeing change initiatives at my organization succeed. 1 2 3 4 5

3. Adequate communication to employees takes place prior to implementing new programs and/or systems. 1 2 3 4 5

4. Information about upcoming changes is delivered in a timely manner. 1 2 3 4 5

5. Change initiatives have helped our organization achieve its growth objectives. 1 2 3 4 5

6. This organization is making the changes necessary to compete effectively. 1 2 3 4 5

7. Our organization has a real interest in innovation. 1 2 3 4 5

8. Past change initiatives have had positive results. 1 2 3 4 5

9. The climate for change is very positive and supportive in my organization. 1 2 3 4 5

10. Constant improvement is valued by this organization. 1 2 3 4 5

QUESTIONNAIRE 3, Cont'd.

Employee Opinion Survey on Organizational Change

Please identify at least 2 or 3 things that we should be doing to better facilitate change in the organization:

Please identify at least 2 or 3 things that you feel we are doing well in managing change:

Thank you for your time and feedback!

QUESTIONNAIRE 4

Employee Opinion Survey on Employee Engagement

INSTRUCTIONS

This survey was designed to get feedback from you regarding your work experiences at our organization. The results of this survey will enable us to identify what we do well as an organization as well as identify areas that may need improvement. Your responses will be completely anonymous. Survey results will be reported in general terms and will not identify individuals. Please mark the number on the right that best represents your opinion, based on the scale below. Your feedback is greatly appreciated! Please be sure to use the following scale to define your response:

Strongly Disagree	Disagree	Neutral	Agree	Strongly Agree
1	2	3	4	5

1. Considering everything, I am satisfied working for this organization at the present time.　　1　2　3　4　5

2. I am doing something I consider satisfying and worthwhile in my job.　　1　2　3　4　5

3. My job is challenging and interesting.　　1　2　3　4　5

4. I am proud to be part of this organization.　　1　2　3　4　5

5. I am committed to seeing this organization succeed.　　1　2　3　4　5

6. I see myself working for this organization three years from now.　　1　2　3　4　5

7. I am confident we can face the business challenges of the future.　　1　2　3　4　5

8. I am treated with dignity and respect.　　1　2　3　4　5

9. I have the freedom I need to do my job.　　1　2　3　4　5

10. I am involved with decisions that affect my work.　　1　2　3　4　5

11. The work I do is very important to the success of my organization.　　1　2　3　4　5

12. I am expected to produce significant but reasonable results.　　1　2　3　4　5

13. I am satisfied with my opportunity for growth and development.　　1　2　3　4　5

14. I believe my career aspirations can be achieved at this organization.　　1　2　3　4　5

15. I am satisfied with the level of balance between my work and personal life.　　1　2　3　4　5

16. I have the flexibility to arrange my work so that I can meet my business objectives and balance my family and personal needs.　　1　2　3　4　5

QUESTIONNAIRE 4, Cont'd.

Employee Opinion Survey on Employee Engagement

Please identify at least 2 or 3 things that we should be doing to improve as an organization:

Please identify at least 2 or 3 things that you like about working for this organization:

Thank you for your time and feedback!

QUESTIONNAIRE 5

Employee Opinion Survey on Communications

INSTRUCTIONS

This survey was designed to get feedback from you regarding your work experiences at our organization. The results of this survey will enable us to identify what we do well as an organization as well as identify areas that may need improvement. Your responses will be completely anonymous. Survey results will be reported in general terms and will not identify individuals. Please mark the number on the right that best represents your opinion, based on the scale below. Your feedback is greatly appreciated! Please be sure to use the following scale to define your response:

Strongly Disagree	Disagree	Neutral	Agree	Strongly Agree
1	2	3	4	5

1. My manager does a good job of keeping me informed about matters affecting me.   1 2 3 4 5

2. I receive the information I need about changes that affect my work.   1 2 3 4 5

3. Information is communicated in a timely manner.   1 2 3 4 5

4. Information is communicated openly and honestly in this organization.   1 2 3 4 5

5. This organization ensures policies and procedures are easy to understand.   1 2 3 4 5

6. Organizational goals and objectives are clearly explained to me.   1 2 3 4 5

7. I have enough information to do my job well.   1 2 3 4 5

8. Information about our organization's policies, practices, and procedures is easily available.   1 2 3 4 5

9. We are kept informed about important developments in different departments.   1 2 3 4 5

10. We are kept informed about important developments at different work locations.   1 2 3 4 5

11. This organization has adequate procedures for sharing information.   1 2 3 4 5

12. Coworkers share information willingly.   1 2 3 4 5

13. I would feel comfortable communicating openly with senior management if the need arose.   1 2 3 4 5

14. People communicate comfortably with one another in this organization regardless of position or level.   1 2 3 4 5

QUESTIONNAIRE 5, Cont'd.

Employee Opinion Survey on Communications

Please identify at least 2 or 3 things that we should be doing to improve communications as an organization:

Please identify at least 2 or 3 things that you feel work well about our organizational communications:

Thank you for your time and feedback!

QUESTIONNAIRE 6

Employee Opinion Survey on Compensation

INSTRUCTIONS

This survey was designed to get feedback from you regarding your work experiences at our organization. The results of this survey will enable us to identify what we do well as an organization as well as identify areas that may need improvement. Your responses will be completely anonymous. Survey results will be reported in general terms and will not identify individuals. Please mark the number on the right that best represents your opinion, based on the scale below. Your feedback is greatly appreciated! Please be sure to use the following scale to define your response:

Strongly Disagree	Disagree	Neutral	Agree	Strongly Agree
1	2	3	4	5

1. My total pay is adequate compared to other's in this organization.   1 2 3 4 5

2. Compensation practices at this organization are fair and reasonable.   1 2 3 4 5

3. Associates in my department are compensated (pay and benefits) fairly in relation to similar work elsewhere.   1 2 3 4 5

4. This organization pays me fairly for the work I do.   1 2 3 4 5

5. I understand how my compensation is determined.   1 2 3 4 5

6. I feel individuals are compensated appropriately as their responsibilities are increased.   1 2 3 4 5

7. People at this organization are rewarded according to their job performance.   1 2 3 4 5

8. This organization provides appropriate salaries considering duties and responsibilities.   1 2 3 4 5

9. My total earnings are fair considering my duties and responsibilities.   1 2 3 4 5

10. I would prefer an increase in my salary rather than improved or additional benefits.   1 2 3 4 5

QUESTIONNAIRE 6, Cont'd.

Employee Opinion Survey on Compensation

Please identify at least 2 or 3 things that we should be doing to improve compensation systems at our organization:

Please identify at least 2 or 3 things that you feel work well about our compensation system:

Thank you for your time and feedback!

QUESTIONNAIRE 7

Employee Opinion Survey on Coworker Relations

INSTRUCTIONS

This survey was designed to get feedback from you regarding your work experiences at our organization. The results of this survey will enable us to identify what we do well as an organization as well as identify areas that may need improvement. Your responses will be completely anonymous. Survey results will be reported in general terms and will not identify individuals. Please mark the number on the right that best represents your opinion, based on the scale below. Your feedback is greatly appreciated! Please be sure to use the following scale to define your response:

Strongly Disagree	Disagree	Neutral	Agree	Strongly Agree
1	2	3	4	5

1. People are willing to put in as much effort as necessary to get the job done.	1 2 3 4 5
2. People communicate comfortably with one another in this organization.	1 2 3 4 5
3. I get the cooperation I need from people outside my department.	1 2 3 4 5
4. The people I work with are friendly and helpful.	1 2 3 4 5
5. Employees in my organization generally trust one another and offer support.	1 2 3 4 5
6. The level of competitiveness within our organization is appropriate.	1 2 3 4 5
7. Employees in my department treat others with dignity and respect.	1 2 3 4 5
8. Employees in my department want to participate in important decisions that affect their work.	1 2 3 4 5
9. My coworkers have adequate training for the jobs they do.	1 2 3 4 5
10. People here seem committed to helping the organization succeed.	1 2 3 4 5
11. People participate willingly in efforts to improve performance in the department (quality, production, cost effectiveness, etc.).	1 2 3 4 5
12. People in my department understand that their actions have impact on the bottom line.	1 2 3 4 5
13. People in my department feel their time and efforts are used effectively.	1 2 3 4 5
14. People I work with help each other out when problems arise.	1 2 3 4 5

QUESTIONNAIRE 7, Cont'd.

Employee Opinion Survey on Coworker Relations

Please identify at least 2 or 3 things that we should be doing to improve coworker relations as an organization:

Please identify at least 2 or 3 aspects of coworker relations in this organization that work well:

Thank you for your time and feedback!

QUESTIONNAIRE 8

Employee Opinion Survey on Fairness and Diversity

INSTRUCTIONS

This survey was designed to get feedback from you regarding your work experiences at our organization. The results of this survey will enable us to identify what we do well as an organization as well as identify areas that may need improvement. Your responses will be completely anonymous. Survey results will be reported in general terms and will not identify individuals. Please mark the number on the right that best represents your opinion, based on the scale below. Your feedback is greatly appreciated! Please be sure to use the following scale to define your response:

Strongly Disagree	Disagree	Neutral	Agree	Strongly Agree
1	2	3	4	5

1. Our organization treats employees fairly without regard to employment level.   1 2 3 4 5

2. All people, regardless of race, nationality, gender, age, or other individual characteristics, are given a fair opportunity to succeed in the organization.   1 2 3 4 5

3. There is a strong drive toward satisfying the needs of all employees in this organization.   1 2 3 4 5

4. Resources are allocated fairly.   1 2 3 4 5

5. I work in an environment where I feel comfortable being myself.   1 2 3 4 5

6. I am encouraged to treat others with dignity and respect.   1 2 3 4 5

7. The level of diversity at [organization name] is appropriate.   1 2 3 4 5

8. [Organization name] values the contributions of people with different work experience.   1 2 3 4 5

9. My work group makes good use of individual differences in style, approach, and skills.   1 2 3 4 5

10. My work group has a climate in which diverse perspectives are valued.   1 2 3 4 5

11. People in my work group communicate comfortably with others regardless of background.   1 2 3 4 5

12. Senior management demonstrates its support for diversity by its actions.   1 2 3 4 5

13. Our organization provides work assignments in a way that is fair to all employees.   1 2 3 4 5

14. This organization encourages a climate where diverse perspectives are valued.   1 2 3 4 5

QUESTIONNAIRE 8, Cont'd.

Employee Opinion Survey on Fairness and Diversity

Please identify at least 2 or 3 things that we should be doing to improve as an organization:

Please identify at least 2 or 3 things that you feel we do well as an organization:

Thank you for your time and feedback!

QUESTIONNAIRE 9

Employee Opinion Survey on the Individual Employee's Manager

INSTRUCTIONS

This survey was designed to get feedback from you regarding your work experiences with your manager at our organization. The results of this survey will enable us to identify what we do well as an organization as well as identify areas that may need improvement. Your responses will be completely anonymous. Survey results will be reported in general terms and will not identify individuals. Please mark the number on the right that best represents your opinion, based on the scale below. Your feedback is greatly appreciated! Please be sure to use the following scale to define your response:

Strongly Disagree	Disagree	Neutral	Agree	Strongly Agree
1	2	3	4	5

1. My manager is fair in dealing with people.		1 2 3 4 5
2. My manager ensures that people who do a good job are recognized and appreciated.		1 2 3 4 5
3. My manager ensures that I am adequately informed about matters affecting me.		1 2 3 4 5
4. My manager gives me adequate feedback on the work I do.		1 2 3 4 5
5. My manager takes a supportive role in my professional growth and development.		1 2 3 4 5
6. My manager encourages me to do a good job.		1 2 3 4 5
7. My manager backs me when necessary.		1 2 3 4 5
8. I would feel comfortable going to my manager with a concern.		1 2 3 4 5
9. My manager helps me overcome barriers to getting the job done.		1 2 3 4 5
10. My manager communicates well with everyone in the department.		1 2 3 4 5
11. My manager involves me in decisions that affect my work.		1 2 3 4 5
12. My manager gives me the freedom I need to do my job.		1 2 3 4 5
13. My manager provides the resources I need to do my job.		1 2 3 4 5
14. My manager sets clear goals and objectives.		1 2 3 4 5
15. It is clear how my manager will evaluate my performance.		1 2 3 4 5
16. My manager sets work objectives that motivate people.		1 2 3 4 5
17. My manager uses good judgment in making decisions.		1 2 3 4 5
18. My manager effectively coordinates the work flow in our department.		1 2 3 4 5
19. My manager makes decisions promptly when needed.		1 2 3 4 5
20. My manager is in control of what is going on in our department.		1 2 3 4 5
21. My manager tries to assign work to maximize productivity.		1 2 3 4 5

QUESTIONNAIRE 9, Cont'd.

Employee Opinion Survey on the Individual Employee's Manager

Please identify at least 2 or 3 suggestions for your manager:

Please identify at least 2 or 3 things that you feel your manager does well:

Thank you for your time and feedback!

QUESTIONNAIRE 10

Employee Opinion Survey on Management

INSTRUCTIONS

This survey was designed to get feedback from you regarding your work experiences at our organization. The results of this survey will enable us to identify what we do well as an organization as well as identify areas that may need improvement. Your responses will be completely anonymous. Survey results will be reported in general terms and will not identify individuals. Please mark the number on the right that best represents your opinion, based on the scale below. Your feedback is greatly appreciated! Please be sure to use the following scale to define your response:

Strongly Disagree	Disagree	Neutral	Agree	Strongly Agree
1	2	3	4	5

1. Top management is fair in dealing with people.		1 2 3 4 5
2. Management in my organization treats me with dignity and respect.		1 2 3 4 5
3. This organization values its employees.		1 2 3 4 5
4. Management will take action based on the results of this survey.		1 2 3 4 5
5. I have trust and confidence in the leadership of this organization.		1 2 3 4 5
6. There is genuine management concern for the problems employees face.		1 2 3 4 5
7. Management thinks creatively.		1 2 3 4 5
8. Management provides a clear picture of the long-term goals and direction of our organization.		1 2 3 4 5
9. Management has the ability to identify new business opportunities.		1 2 3 4 5
10. This organization is well managed.		1 2 3 4 5
11. Management acts consistently; they do as they say.		1 2 3 4 5
12. I would feel comfortable communicating openly with senior management if the need arose.		1 2 3 4 5

QUESTIONNAIRE 10, Cont'd.

Employee Opinion Survey on Management

Please identify at least 2 or 3 suggestions for senior management at this organization:

Please identify at least 2 or 3 things that you feel our senior management does well:

Thank you for your time and feedback!

QUESTIONNAIRE 11

Employee Opinion Survey on Job Satisfaction

INSTRUCTIONS

This survey was designed to get feedback from you regarding your work experiences at our organization. The results of this survey will enable us to identify what we do well as an organization as well as identify areas that may need improvement. Your responses will be completely anonymous. Survey results will be reported in general terms and will not identify individuals. Please mark the number on the right that best represents your opinion, based on the scale below. Your feedback is greatly appreciated! Please be sure to use the following scale to define your response:

Strongly Disagree	Disagree	Neutral	Agree	Strongly Agree
1	2	3	4	5

1. My job makes good use of my skills and abilities.	1 2 3 4 5
2. I receive the training I need to do my job.	1 2 3 4 5
3. I am given opportunities to improve my skills in this organization.	1 2 3 4 5
4. My job is challenging and interesting.	1 2 3 4 5
5. I am doing something I consider satisfying and worthwhile in my job.	1 2 3 4 5
6. My job offers me the opportunity to gain work experience in challenging new areas.	1 2 3 4 5
7. I like my job at this organization.	1 2 3 4 5
8. I understand the link between what I do and the organization's objectives.	1 2 3 4 5
9. The work I do is very important to the success of my organization.	1 2 3 4 5
10. I am doing something I consider really worthwhile.	1 2 3 4 5
11. I really feel I accomplish something each day.	1 2 3 4 5
12. I have personal control over the way my work must be done.	1 2 3 4 5
13. I feel the amount of work required of me is about right.	1 2 3 4 5

QUESTIONNAIRE 11, Cont'd.

Employee Opinion Survey on Job Satisfaction

Please identify at least 2 or 3 things that could be improved about the job you currently do:

Please identify at least 2 or 3 things that you like about your work:

Thank you for your time and feedback!

QUESTIONNAIRE 12

Employee Opinion Survey on Workplace Resources and Safety

INSTRUCTIONS

This survey was designed to get feedback from you regarding your work experiences at our organization. The results of this survey will enable us to identify what we do well as an organization as well as identify areas that may need improvement. Your responses will be completely anonymous. Survey results will be reported in general terms and will not identify individuals. Please mark the number on the right that best represents your opinion, based on the scale below. Your feedback is greatly appreciated! Please be sure to use the following scale to define your response:

Strongly Disagree	Disagree	Neutral	Agree	Strongly Agree
1	2	3	4	5

1. I am clear about safety standards related to my work.   1 2 3 4 5

2. Safety standards are always followed.   1 2 3 4 5

3. I feel the amount of work required of me is about right.   1 2 3 4 5

4. My work environment enables me to be as productive as I can be.   1 2 3 4 5

5. I have enough information to do my job well.   1 2 3 4 5

6. The equipment provided is adequate.   1 2 3 4 5

7. I have the resources I need to do my job.   1 2 3 4 5

8. I receive the training I need to do my job.   1 2 3 4 5

9. I get the cooperation I need from those outside my department.   1 2 3 4 5

10. The physical security of my organization's facility is adequate.   1 2 3 4 5

11. Associates in my department make responsible decisions regarding the safety and welfare of themselves and others.   1 2 3 4 5

12. I know what procedure to follow in the event of an emergency.   1 2 3 4 5

QUESTIONNAIRE 12, Cont'd.

Employee Opinion Survey on Workplace Resources and Safety

Please identify at least 2 or 3 things that we should be doing to improve safety as an organization:

Please identify what we do well with regard to maintaining a safe and secure work environment:

Thank you for your time and feedback!

Chapter 5

Mission Alignment Surveys

WHAT'S IN THIS CHAPTER?

- Questionnaire 13. Employee Opinion Survey on Organizational Mission and Values
- Questionnaire 14. Employee Opinion Survey on Innovation and Creativity
- Questionnaire 15. Employee Opinion Survey on Quality Practices
- Questionnaire 16. Employee Opinion Survey on Customer Care
- Questionnaire 17. Employee Opinion Survey on Ethics

MISSION ALIGNMENT SURVEYS measure whether an organization's stated mission, vision, and values are embraced and practiced by all levels. Since they must be based on organization-specific statements, these surveys are often customized. Nonetheless, experience has shown that certain mission alignment questions come up again and again and can be used generically.

Two key internal sources tend to cause interference with an organization's mission:

- Managers and executives are insufficiently effective at delivering and reinforcing the message.
- Employees don't find the message practical or credible.

The employee surveys in this chapter diagnose gaps between stated mission and actual practice.

Organizational Mission and Values

The Employee Opinion Survey on Organizational Mission and Values addresses the gap that many employees see between stated mission and actual practice. It also can be used to diagnose the extent to which respondents feel the presence of a mission, vision, or values.

When to Use

This is a good general tool for diagnosing mission alignment. It also gauges morale effectively, as strong negative responses to the statements show disenfranchisement and disillusionment. Other symptoms include the following:

- Widely questioned business decisions

- Employees who don't know what's required to support the organization's mission

- Employees who feel poorly informed by senior management and are unclear about organization goals, strategies, plans, or policies

- Employees who comment on the gap between stated mission and values and the actions of management and coworkers

Considerations

The terms *mission* and *values* may need some explanation in a cover memo or other communication. If business strategy is going to change within six months, consider adding some "change readiness" elements to this questionnaire. (See Chapter Four.) Also, it may not be a good time to do a survey at all.

Questionnaire 13. Employee Opinion Survey on Organizational Mission and Values

1. Senior management gives employees a clear picture of the direction in which our organization is headed.

2. I have adequate knowledge of our organization's vision, mission, values, and objectives.

3. The actions of my coworkers support our organization's mission and values.

4. I can see a clear link between my work and the organization's objectives.

5. I know how my job supports the overall goals of the organization.

6. I have a clear understanding of my role, relationships, and responsibilities.

7. I understand how my work fits into the overall objectives of our organization.

8. My manager demonstrates through his or her actions a commitment to our mission, values, and operating principles.

9. Senior management frequently refers to our values and how they relate to our business.

10. My manager acts in a way that is consistent with the stated values.

11. Senior management frequently refers to our values and how they relate to our business.

12. I know and understand our values.

13. There is a high degree of involvement and positive energy in this organization.

Innovation and Creativity

The Employee Opinion Survey on Innovation and Creativity measures whether the key elements needed for an innovative atmosphere are present:

- Creative group thinking and problem solving

- Individual creative thinking and problem solving

- Recognition of creative thinking and problem solving

When to Use

If the organization's environment or market demands creativity and problem solving, this questionnaire will help assess respondents' readiness to generate innovative new approaches, products, and services. Other symptoms that indicate a need for this questionnaire include the following:

- Pessimism about the organization's approach to its market

- Employees who feel that change is required but not encouraged

- People who offer creative solutions become discouraged or leave

- Little initiative on the part of employees

Considerations

This survey addresses idea generation, not necessarily change readiness. Although new ideas often lead to changes, the Employee Opinion Survey on Innovation and Change is a good instrument for measuring organizational flexibility, openness to new ideas, and adaptability.

Questionnaire 14. Employee Opinion Survey on Innovation and Creativity

1. People are encouraged to try new ways of doing things.

2. I have the ability to challenge the way things are done.

3. Employees are encouraged to offer their opinions and ideas.

4. I am given an opportunity to present and try new ideas.

5. I feel encouraged to come up with new and better ways of doing things.

6. This organization recognizes those who come up with new ideas.

7. Employees are encouraged to participate in solving work-related problems.

8. Management is genuinely interested in employee ideas on how to improve our products and services.

9. In general, I am very satisfied with the amount of opportunity I have to try new ideas.

10. This organization encourages diverse perspectives when looking for ways to solve problems.

11. The people who are valued most in this organization are those who come up with new ideas.

12. Our organization values people who turn ideas into action.

Quality Practices

This survey focuses on the ability of an organization to deliver products or services at a consistent standard. The survey can be used as a preliminary assessment for organizations pursuing quality certifications, such as Baldrige or ISO awards. Generally, though, the measures required to support these certifications are more rigorous than the one presented here.

When to Use

The Employee Opinion Survey on Quality Practices is an excellent precursor to quality initiatives. It may also be used to determine whether quality initiatives are needed, though this is often obvious from other sources. You will measure perceptions of quality orientation among coworkers, managers, and the workforce in general. Symptoms addressed by this questionnaire include:

- Low performance standards, with production quality not up to expectations or standards

- Lack of pride in products

Considerations

The people closest to the work will have the best ideas about needed changes. Pay particular attention to open-ended comments.

Questionnaire 15. Employee Opinion Survey on Quality Practices

1. People here are really committed to producing high-quality work.

2. People in my department take pride in doing a good job.

3. Our work group has clear quality standards.

4. Our work group has clear measures to support the quality standards.

5. My work group is effective in producing high-quality work.

6. My work group maintains high standards of performance.

7. The example set by fellow employees encourages me to produce high-quality work.

8. People in my department have made significant improvements in the way we do our jobs within the past six months.

9. People appropriately balance concern for productivity with concern for quality.

10. Employees in this organization have a strong commitment to producing high-quality work.

11. My manager clearly communicates both short- and long-term quality goals.

12. Senior management is committed to producing high-quality work output.

Customer Care

Many organizations have routine customer satisfaction surveys. But how many survey their employees about customer care? The results of this questionnaire can create a baseline and ongoing measurements of employee beliefs about the organization's commitment to customers and focus on the market.

When to Use

The Employee Opinion Survey on Customer Care is usually used in combination with an external customer survey. Some symptoms that it addresses include:

- Employees who view the organization as ineffective in its market-place and widely question business decisions
- Poor customer focus leads to service or product defects
- Poor retention of customers
- Employees who are disturbed by product or service quality

Considerations

You should balance employees' views of the organization's focus on customers with data and input from the marketplace. Generally this survey is given only to employees who have direct customer contact.

Questionnaire 16. Employee Opinion Survey on Customer Care

1. We listen to the needs of our customers.
2. We provide a very high quality of service to our customers.
3. Management is aware of marketplace trends.
4. We make customer satisfaction a primary concern of all employees.
5. We select high-quality vendors and suppliers.
6. We have developed a quality level in our products/services that customers trust.
7. We continuously study customer needs and expectations.
8. We keep customers satisfied by resolving complaints quickly and ethically.
9. We compare our customer satisfaction levels with those of our competitors.
10. We change products and services to meet customer preferences.
11. We keep present and potential customers in mind while planning for the future.
12. Associates in my department work to improve our organization's reputation for its products and services.

Ethics

The Employee Opinion Survey on Ethics can be used to detect the practice of ethical behavior and the organization's general ethical atmosphere. When scores show neutral to strong disagreement, be concerned that employees are witnessing ethical lapses. You may receive comments that require follow-up. Bringing up a topic and then not doing something about the problems that surface may have legal implications.

When to Use

This survey works best as part of a routine survey effort or combined with other survey topics. It can also be used as a quick barometer of the atmosphere for honesty and freedom from fear of retaliation. Symptoms include the following:

- Employees who are disturbed by the lack of quality of products and services

- A sense among some employees that products are not meeting the organization's marketing promises

- Employees who do not feel free to discuss sensitive topics or report violations because of a of fear retaliation

- An atmosphere of suspiciousness and mistrust

Considerations

Used as a stand-alone survey, this questionnaire will almost surely raise concerns that management is seeking out "culprits." To avoid this concern, use it on a routine basis or combine it with another questionnaire. Be sure to have a minimum of five respondents to lessen concerns that the survey sponsor is looking for a scapegoat. Don't ask a question unless the organization can do something about negative findings.

Questionnaire 17. Employee Opinion Survey on Ethics

1. I feel that I could report, without fear of retaliation, an ethical violation in my organization.

2. I have confidence that management will respond appropriately to any ethical concerns that are brought to their attention.

3. My manager responds appropriately to any ethical concerns that are brought to his or her attention.

4. Management in this organization behaves in an ethical manner.

5. Associates in my department act responsibly and ethically in how we treat each other.

6. My manager acts in a way that is consistent with the stated values.

7. Overall, we live up to our organizational values.

8. There is consistency in what we stand for and how we act.

9. I know and understand the values of this organization.

10. This organization keeps customers satisfied by resolving complaints quickly and ethically.

•   •   •

The surveys in this chapter address goals or aspirations of organizations. In the next chapter are three surveys designed for specific moments in the employment of individuals.

QUESTIONNAIRE 13

Employee Opinion Survey on Organizational Mission and Values

INSTRUCTIONS

This survey was designed to get feedback from you regarding your work experiences at our organization. The results of this survey will enable us to identify what we do well as an organization as well as identify areas that may need improvement. Your responses will be completely anonymous. Survey results will be reported in general terms and will not identify individuals. Please mark the number on the right that best represents your opinion, based on the scale below. Your feedback is greatly appreciated! Please be sure to use the following scale to define your response:

Strongly Disagree	Disagree	Neutral	Agree	Strongly Agree
1	2	3	4	5

1. Senior management gives employees a clear picture of the direction in which our organization is headed.   1 2 3 4 5

2. I have adequate knowledge of our organization's vision, mission, values, and objectives.   1 2 3 4 5

3. The actions of my coworkers support our organization's mission and values.   1 2 3 4 5

4. I can see a clear link between my work and the organization's objectives.   1 2 3 4 5

5. I know how my job supports the overall goals of the organization.   1 2 3 4 5

6. I have a clear understanding of my role, relationships, and responsibilities.   1 2 3 4 5

7. I understand how my work fits into the overall objectives of our organization.   1 2 3 4 5

8. My manager demonstrates through his or her actions a commitment to our mission, values, and operating principles.   1 2 3 4 5

9. Senior management frequently refers to our values and how they relate to our business.   1 2 3 4 5

10. My manager acts in a way that is consistent with the stated values.   1 2 3 4 5

11. Senior management frequently refers to our values and how they relate to our business.   1 2 3 4 5

12. I know and understand our values.   1 2 3 4 5

13. There is a high degree of involvement and positive energy in this organization.   1 2 3 4 5

QUESTIONNAIRE 13, Cont'd.

Employee Opinion Survey on Organizational Mission and Values

Please identify at least 2 or 3 things that we should be doing to improve your ability to understand and practice our values:

Please identify at least 2 or 3 things that make you feel we successfully put our mission and values into action:

Thank you for your time and feedback!

QUESTIONNAIRE 14

Employee Opinion Survey on Innovation and Creativity

INSTRUCTIONS

This survey was designed to get feedback from you regarding your work experiences at our organization. The results of this survey will enable us to identify what we do well as an organization as well as identify areas that may need improvement. Your responses will be completely anonymous. Survey results will be reported in general terms and will not identify individuals. Please mark the number on the right that best represents your opinion, based on the scale below. Your feedback is greatly appreciated! Please be sure to use the following scale to define your response:

Strongly Disagree	Disagree	Neutral	Agree	Strongly Agree
1	2	3	4	5

1. People are encouraged to try new ways of doing things.	1 2 3 4 5
2. I have the ability to challenge the way things are done.	1 2 3 4 5
3. Employees are encouraged to offer their opinions and ideas.	1 2 3 4 5
4. I am given an opportunity to present and try new ideas.	1 2 3 4 5
5. I feel encouraged to come up with new and better ways of doing things.	1 2 3 4 5
6. This organization recognizes those who come up with new ideas.	1 2 3 4 5
7. Employees are encouraged to participate in solving work-related problems.	1 2 3 4 5
8. Management is genuinely interested in employee ideas on how to improve our products and services.	1 2 3 4 5
9. In general, I am very satisfied with the amount of opportunity I have to try new ideas.	1 2 3 4 5
10. This organization encourages diverse perspectives when looking for ways to solve problems.	1 2 3 4 5
11. The people who are valued most in this organization are those who come up with new ideas.	1 2 3 4 5
12. Our organization values people who turn ideas into action.	1 2 3 4 5

QUESTIONNAIRE 14, Cont'd.

Employee Opinion Survey on Innovation and Creativity

Please identify at least 2 or 3 things that we should be doing to improve innovation within our organization:

Please identify at least 2 or 3 things that we do to support an atmosphere for innovation and creativity:

Thank you for your time and feedback!

QUESTIONNAIRE 15

Employee Opinion Survey on Quality Practices

INSTRUCTIONS

This survey was designed to get feedback from you regarding quality practices at our organization. The results of this survey will enable us to identify what we do well as an organization as well as identify areas that may need improvement. Your responses will be completely anonymous. Survey results will be reported in general terms and will not identify individuals. Please mark the number on the right that best represents your opinion, based on the scale below. Your feedback is greatly appreciated! Please be sure to use the following scale to define your response:

Strongly Disagree	Disagree	Neutral	Agree	Strongly Agree
1	2	3	4	5

1. People here are really committed to producing high-quality work.   1 2 3 4 5

2. People in my department take pride in doing a good job.   1 2 3 4 5

3. Our work group has clear quality standards.   1 2 3 4 5

4. Our work group has clear measures to support the quality standards.   1 2 3 4 5

5. My work group is effective in producing high-quality work.   1 2 3 4 5

6. My work group maintains high standards of performance.   1 2 3 4 5

7. The example set by fellow employees encourages me to produce high-quality work.   1 2 3 4 5

8. People in my department have made significant improvements in the way we do our jobs within the past six months.   1 2 3 4 5

9. People appropriately balance concern for productivity with concern for quality.   1 2 3 4 5

10. Employees in this organization have a strong commitment to producing high-quality work.   1 2 3 4 5

11. My manager clearly communicates both short- and long-term quality goals.   1 2 3 4 5

12. Senior management is committed to producing high-quality work output.   1 2 3 4 5

QUESTIONNAIRE 15, Cont'd.

Employee Opinion Survey on Quality Practices

Please identify at least 2 or 3 things that we should be doing to improve quality as an organization:

Please identify at least 2 or 3 quality practices that we do well:

Thank you for your time and feedback!

QUESTIONNAIRE 16

Employee Opinion Survey on Customer Care

INSTRUCTIONS

This survey was designed to get feedback from you regarding your work experiences at our organization. The results of this survey will enable us to identify what we do well as an organization as well as identify areas that may need improvement. Your responses will be completely anonymous. Survey results will be reported in general terms and will not identify individuals. Please mark the number on the right that best represents your opinion, based on the scale below. Your feedback is greatly appreciated! Please be sure to use the following scale to define your response:

Strongly Disagree	Disagree	Neutral	Agree	Strongly Agree
1	2	3	4	5

1. We listen to the needs of our customers.	1 2 3 4 5
2. We provide a very high quality of service to our customers.	1 2 3 4 5
3. Management is aware of marketplace trends.	1 2 3 4 5
4. We make customer satisfaction a primary concern of all employees.	1 2 3 4 5
5. We select high-quality vendors and suppliers.	1 2 3 4 5
6. We have developed a quality level in our products/services that customers trust.	1 2 3 4 5
7. We continuously study customer needs and expectations.	1 2 3 4 5
8. We keep customers satisfied by resolving complaints quickly and ethically.	1 2 3 4 5
9. We compare our customer satisfaction levels with those of our competitors.	1 2 3 4 5
10. We change products and services to meet customer preferences.	1 2 3 4 5
11. We keep present and potential customers in mind while planning for the future.	1 2 3 4 5
12. Associates in my department work to improve our organization's reputation for its products and services.	1 2 3 4 5

QUESTIONNAIRE 16, Cont'd.

Employee Opinion Survey on Customer Care

Please identify at least 2 or 3 things that we should be doing to improve customer care:

Please identify at least 2 or 3 customer care practices that we do well:

Thank you for your time and feedback!

QUESTIONNAIRE 17

Employee Opinion Survey on Ethics

INSTRUCTIONS

This survey was designed to get feedback from you regarding your work experiences at our organization. The results of this survey will enable us to identify what we do well as an organization as well as identify areas that may need improvement. Your responses will be completely anonymous. Survey results will be reported in general terms and will not identify individuals. Please mark the number on the right that best represents your opinion, based on the scale below. Your feedback is greatly appreciated! Please be sure to use the following scale to define your response:

Strongly Disagree	Disagree	Neutral	Agree	Strongly Agree
1	2	3	4	5

1. I feel that I could report, without fear of retaliation, an ethical violation in my organization.   1 2 3 4 5

2. I have confidence that management will respond appropriately to any ethical concerns that are brought to their attention.   1 2 3 4 5

3. My manager responds appropriately to any ethical concerns that are brought to his or her attention.   1 2 3 4 5

4. Management in this organization behaves in an ethical manner.   1 2 3 4 5

5. Associates in my department act responsibly and ethically in how we treat each other.   1 2 3 4 5

6. My manager acts in a way that is consistent with the stated values.   1 2 3 4 5

7. Overall, we live up to our organizational values.   1 2 3 4 5

8. There is consistency in what we stand for and how we act.   1 2 3 4 5

9. I know and understand the values of this organization.   1 2 3 4 5

10. This organization keeps customers satisfied by resolving complaints quickly and ethically.   1 2 3 4 5

QUESTIONNAIRE 17, Cont'd.

Employee Opinion Survey on Ethics

Please identify at least 2 or 3 things that we should be doing to improve ethical practices as an organization:

Please identify at least 2 or 3 ways in which we successfully practice ethical values:

Thank you for your time and feedback!

Chapter 6
Event-Related Surveys

WHAT'S IN THIS CHAPTER?

- Questionnaire 18. New Employee Survey
- Questionnaire 19. Exit Survey
- Questionnaire 20. Training Effectiveness Survey

THREE KEY EVENTS in an individual employee's time with an organization are posthire, posttraining, and voluntary termination. This chapter provides some templates for tracking opinions about these events. The questionnaires in this chapter are provided as examples and may need customization. (See Chapter Eight on questionnaire development.)

The three surveys examined here differ from all the others in this book in a key way: respondents may not be assured of anonymity. For instance, a small- to medium-size employer may have only a handful of terminations in a quarter or a year. The same could be true of newly hired employees and training attendees. As a result, it is often impossible to promise complete anonymity.

Nevertheless, you can promise confidentiality. For instance, provide one collection point for the feedback, such as a human resource person or an outside vendor, or promise that the respondents' answers will be presented to management only when they can be grouped with at least four other responses. A promise of confidentiality that can be backed up with a sincere set of procedures will go a long way toward getting responses.

New Employee Survey

This questionnaire assesses a new employee's early experiences with the company. Experts agree that the first few months of employment can establish a perspective that is difficult to change. If that first impression is positive, the employee is somewhat "inoculated" against later less favorable experiences, should they arise. If the first impression is negative, the employee often becomes difficult to motivate and is at risk for quick turnover.

When to Use

This survey is best done between one and two months after a new employee has joined the organization. This allows the person enough time to complete orientation programs and become acclimated. A new employee survey may contain the following elements, plus as many others as needed:

- How the person was referred
- Whether the recruiting function was professional and effective
- What attracted the employee to the organization
- Whether sufficient time, attention, and information were given to the new employee during the induction process
- Whether the job turned out to be as described during recruitment
- Information on the employee's demographics

Questionnaire 18, New Employee Survey, provided at the end of this chapter, includes all of these suggested elements.

Considerations

This survey may require substantial customization, depending on the features of the orientation period.

Exit Survey

Exit surveys represent an attempt to understand whether the loss of a good employee was avoidable. Their main purpose is to uncover problems that might lead to further unwanted turnover if they are not addressed.

When to Use

An exit survey for voluntary turnover is best done between one and three months after the employee has left. The person will likely have started a new position and feel more comfortable about the choice. At this point, employees are more likely to cite factors they might have hesitated to mention before. The timing and method of exit surveys have a lot of impact on response rate. Many organizations do live interviews, which have certain advantages. One is that they get the highest response rate. Some companies even use this survey as an opportunity to renegotiate the employee's decision to leave. If the information is collected with this objective, however, it should be considered less reliable than data collected purely for survey purposes.

Considerations

Questionnaire 19, Exit Survey, provided at the end of this chapter, is an example of an exit survey. You will probably need to customize it using the CD-ROM. Also, it is written strictly for voluntary terminations and is not appropriate for layoffs or other involuntary terminations.

Training Effectiveness Survey

The Training Effectiveness Survey (Questionnaire 20) is an example of a management development training evaluation survey. It focuses on the attendee's reactions to the training event and asks the attendee to self-assess whether he or she has been able to apply any new skills. This questionnaire may not be sufficient to determine whether the desired behavior or skill changes were actually accomplished. It also does not address the business impact of training. Both of these topics need to be studied in other ways.

When to Use

The survey is best used between one week and one month after training, as it asks questions about on-the-job applications of the training. If the purpose is to measure satisfaction with a specific training event, the survey should be used on the same day or within one week of the event.

Considerations

There are many different types of training and a number of different ways to evaluate its effectiveness. Questionnaire 20, Training Effectiveness Survey, provided at the end of this chapter, is one example of one type of evaluation.

QUESTIONNAIRE 18

New Employee Survey

We are interested in getting your feedback on our employee recruitment and entry/orientation process. Thanks in advance for taking the time to respond. Your feedback will allow us to continuously improve our recruitment and retention efforts.

Please circle the source of your referral for this job:

1. Employee referral

2. Job fair

3. Open house

4. Print advertisement

5. Outplacement firm

6. Internet

7. Unsolicited résumé

8. College/university—alumni

9. Prior experience with the organization as a vendor

10. Rehire, have worked for the organization before

11. Internal job move

12. Other:

For questions 13–21, please respond to each statement according to the following scale:

Strongly Disagree	Disagree	Neutral	Agree	Strongly Agree
1	2	3	4	5

13. The recruiter(s) provided me with sufficient information about this organization to get a good understanding of the operation.   1 2 3 4 5

14. The selection process (appointments, interview schedules, etc.) was handled efficiently and effectively.   1 2 3 4 5

15. The position information provided an accurate description of the work I am actually doing now.   1 2 3 4 5

16. I met key people, with whom I would be working, during the orientation process.   1 2 3 4 5

17. The orientation process accelerated my learning about the business.   1 2 3 4 5

18. I received an orientation to my department (e.g., a facility tour, supply locations, additional responsibility information).   1 2 3 4 5

QUESTIONNAIRE 18, Cont'd.

New Employee Survey

19. My manager was readily available to me.	1 2 3 4 5
20. Sufficient tools and resources were made available to begin the job.	1 2 3 4 5
21. I received sufficient information about benefits.	1 2 3 4 5

For questions 22–32, please respond to each statement by rating the importance of each factor as you considered your decision to join this organization:

Not at all Important	Slightly Important	Somewhat Important	Very Important	Extremely Important
1	2	3	4	5

22. Salary package	1 2 3 4 5
23. Benefits (excluding financial incentives)	1 2 3 4 5
24. Career opportunities	1 2 3 4 5
25. Industry	1 2 3 4 5
26. Culture of the organization	1 2 3 4 5
27. Quality of your prospective boss	1 2 3 4 5
28. Career opportunities	1 2 3 4 5
29. Opportunity to make significant contribution (level of responsibility)	1 2 3 4 5
30. Industry	1 2 3 4 5
31. Level and scope of the position you were offered	1 2 3 4 5
32. Other factors:	

QUESTIONNAIRE 18, Cont'd.

New Employee Survey

33. How does our organization compare with others (based on previous offers, employment experiences, etc.)? Please be specific.

34. How would you rate this organization's performance against the criteria you selected it on, based on your experiences up to now?

Thank you for your time and feedback!

QUESTIONNAIRE 19

Exit Survey

We are interested in learning more about your decision to leave our organization recently. Your responses will help us in our efforts to continuously improve our workplace. In the three sections below, please follow the instructions for describing your decision to leave. We appreciate your feedback. Please be assured your responses will be kept confidential.

Please give up to three of the most important factors in your decision to leave. Circle up to three of the reasons below:

Didn't like the job

Functions/responsibilities

Physical environment/working conditions

Physical safety and security of work environment

Tools, equipment, resources to get job done

Job schedule/work hours

Performance expectations/workload

Product or service quality

Recognition

Training

Position redefined/eliminated

Issues with fairness

Supervisor/manager

Coworkers

Benefits

Compensation, wages/salary

Communication

Corporate culture

Opportunities for personal/career growth

Personal health

Care of family member

Child care availability

Transportation (e.g., length of commute, parking)

Career change

Relocation

Retirement

Return to school

Other: _____

QUESTIONNAIRE 19, Cont'd.

Exit Survey

Please indicate your agreement or disagreement with each of the following statements:

Strongly Disagree	Disagree	Neutral	Agree	Strongly Agree
1	2	3	4	5

This job was a good match for my skills and experiences.   1 2 3 4 5

I had clear goals and objectives for my job.   1 2 3 4 5

The methods and standards that were used to measure my performance were reasonable.   1 2 3 4 5

I received the training I needed to do my job well.   1 2 3 4 5

I received effective performance feedback from my supervisor on a regular basis.   1 2 3 4 5

I had all the information I needed to do my job well.   1 2 3 4 5

The work I was doing was challenging.   1 2 3 4 5

My direct supervisor treated me fairly and with respect.   1 2 3 4 5

I was provided with the flexibility needed to balance the demands of my work and personal life.   1 2 3 4 5

I had opportunities for career advancement within the organization.   1 2 3 4 5

The benefits at the organization are competitive with other companies'.   1 2 3 4 5

I was adequately compensated while I was employed at the organization.   1 2 3 4 5

I was adequately recognized for my contributions.   1 2 3 4 5

My supervisor did a good job of managing people.   1 2 3 4 5

Overall, the morale level in my department was good.   1 2 3 4 5

I would recommend the organization to a friend as a place to work.   1 2 3 4 5

I had another job when I left my position.   Yes   No

QUESTIONNAIRE 19, Cont'd.

Exit Survey

What suggestions or comments do you have that would improve this organization and help retain quality people?

Thank you for your time and feedback!

QUESTIONNAIRE 20

Training Effectiveness Survey

PARTICIPANT INSTRUCTIONS

We are interested in your reactions to the training you have just completed. We are interested in how well you feel you'll be able to apply what you have learned on the job. Your responses are greatly appreciated and will be very helpful to us in planning future sessions.

1. Which **one** of the following has been your primary reason for attending our training courses?

    1. Personal interest

    2. Manager suggested it

    3. It was required

    4. Coworker or peer suggested it

    5. Other:

For questions 2–10, please respond to each statement according to the following scale:

Strongly Disagree	Disagree	Neutral	Agree	Strongly Agree
1	2	3	4	5

2. I am satisfied with the management development training courses that I have attended. 1 2 3 4 5

3. I had sufficient knowledge or skill in the areas covered by these courses before I attended. 1 2 3 4 5

4. I have had the opportunity to use the knowledge and/or skills presented in the training courses. 1 2 3 4 5

5. My confidence in using the knowledge and/or skills presented has increased. 1 2 3 4 5

6. Management has encouraged me to apply the knowledge and/or skills learned from the training courses. 1 2 3 4 5

7. My manager has coached me on how to apply the knowledge and/or skills learned on the job. 1 2 3 4 5

8. I have successfully generated new ideas as a result of attending management development courses. 1 2 3 4 5

9. The management development training courses have helped me perform my job more effectively. 1 2 3 4 5

10. I would recommend this course to others. 1 2 3 4 5

QUESTIONNAIRE 20, Cont'd.

Training Effectiveness Survey

11. What suggestions do you have for improving our training programs?

12. Please comment on what you found to be most valuable about this training program.

Thank you for your time and feedback!

Chapter 7

Planning the Survey

WHAT'S IN THIS CHAPTER?

- How Do We Assign Responsibility for the Survey?
- How Do We Select Respondents?
- How Can We Build Anonymity and Confidentiality into the Process?
- How Should We Plan the Feedback Phase?
- How Can We Win Support from Managers Whose Departments Are Included?
- What Should We Say in an Awareness Campaign?

SOME CHOICES, DECISIONS, and commitments are best made *before* the survey. When the questions we look at here are asked and answered before they arise, surveys go more smoothly.

How Do We Assign Responsibility for the Survey?

Whether you're doing a large, formal survey or a quick questionnaire, the first step is to define roles and responsibilities and to communicate them to the people who must be involved. Successful surveys require a lot of collaboration. In fact, that's one of their main values.

When the data have been collected, the survey process and results provide a focal point for discussion. In a very large organization, the survey team may have as many as ten people. In smaller firms or with shorter surveys, one or two individuals may share all of the roles. Even in a relatively small organization, a steering team can bring perspective, support, resources, and commitment to the project. Here are some key roles and their definitions.

Sponsor

The sponsor has organizational responsibilities broad enough to take action on the survey results. This person may or may not be the originator of the push to conduct the survey, but he or she nevertheless must embrace and promote it. Typically, sponsors are line managers with operational responsibilities.

Spokesperson

Typically the spokesperson is also the sponsor. He or she must be perceived as the person who is best placed to take action on the results.

Steering Team

Quick, focused surveys don't usually require their own steering team, but formal, full-length employee surveys often have one. The need for a steering team is often proportional to the complexity of the questions and the size of the respondent group. If the questionnaire covers only one or two topics and all respondents are from a single work unit or division, a steering team is probably not necessary. As complexity increases, the need increases for multiple voices during the planning phase. This team is typically chaired by the sponsor-spokesperson and directed by a human resource person acting as project manager. Other steering team members are cross-functional management representatives from each division, as well as human resource representatives.

Survey Project Manager

Whether the survey is small or large, this is the one job that must be assigned. It is a key position. With formal, full-length surveys, this is typically a human resource person. For shorter surveys, it may be a department manager, his or her assistant, a member of a project team, or many other people, including a human resource professional. The project manager manages the entire project flow, from planning through follow-up. He or she works with the survey sponsor as well as the survey's other contact people and may serve as director of the steering team, if there is one.

Project Coordinators

In very large operations, there may be a need for project coordinators at locations. They take responsibility for local implementation and feedback.

Feedback Leaders

These are typically department managers who provide the results and gather reactions. In a small survey with a limited audience, the survey sponsor or spokesperson may also be the feedback leader.

How Do We Select Respondents?

For short, focused surveys, selecting respondents is often simple. On occasion, though, giving a small survey can be like giving a small wedding: Who should be invited to complete a survey? Which groups should answer the survey? Should everyone within those groups be surveyed?

Here's a simple rule of thumb for inclusion: if the organization can share results with a group and take action based on a group's responses, they are good candidates for inclusion. If for any reason the organization won't be able to share the results and take action on a group's input, they are poor candidates for inclusion. In fact, the survey might harm relations with those employees, who may view the survey as a waste of time.

Exclusion is more likely to be an issue with short, focused surveys. For instance, an organization was going to make a major software installation that would significantly change the work processes of several large work groups within a division. It wanted to measure the climate for change, assessing readiness to accept the new methods within the groups that would be most directly affected. This meant excluding some departments within the division, an exclusion that elicited some negative comments. The organization defended the choice by saying it would survey only groups whose work was directly affected and whose comments could be directly addressed during the transition.

It is sometimes tricky to ask for responses from one department or division but not another. The lack of an acceptable public explanation for excluding one group may tempt some to include questionable groups anyway. We encourage you to avoid this tendency. If some groups should be excluded, exclude them, but be prepared to offer a good explanation. In the example already given of the software installation, the survey sponsor put the reasons in the letter announcing the survey: "This survey is being distributed only to those departments and work units that will be involved with Phase One of the new software implementation. Additional surveys may be made as Phases Two and Three occur next year."

Alternatively, you might change the survey questions to fit all the groups that must be included.

How Can We Build Anonymity and Confidentiality into the Process?

Respondents often wonder how the data and resulting reports will be used. They ask: "How will my identity be protected?" and "Can my responses be revealed when the data are analyzed?"

If these questions can't be answered clearly and safeguards can't be promised sincerely, it may be best to do no survey at all, for two reasons: respondent uncertainty results in lower response rates, and a question implies a promise of action. If action can't be taken, the negative memory of the survey can exacerbate other management problems.

If the survey is being done under stressful circumstances, recognize the difficulties. For example, one survey sponsor wrote, "Although we have experienced significant layoffs in recent months, it is important that those of us who remain have the resources we need to get the job done. This is one of the ways we can understand how to rebuild our organization."

Confidentiality of results must be addressed. Handle this by showing the safeguards and promising that confidentiality will be honored. This is usually handled during the awareness campaign before and during the survey. These campaigns are important to the survey's outcome, and we explore them in some depth later in this chapter. For instance, in one awareness campaign letter, a manager wrote the following: "You may wonder why we ask so many questions about you, such as your location and length of employment. These are to help us produce reports that we will all find useful in understanding our workplace culture. We will not produce reports for any category where fewer than five responses are received. You have my promise that neither I nor the survey project team will relate responses to any one individual." The success of a survey has everything to do with respondents' confidence about their anonymity in the process and the confidentiality of data. Both response rate and candor are affected.

When it comes to delivering on the promise of confidentiality, there is no substitute for a third party. Even if you are creating and processing the survey yourself, you may still want to use an outside survey firm as the data collection agent. This firm can be asked to return the data in a format that ensures anonymity.

In addition to data collection, privacy must be protected throughout the survey process. Reports must not reveal the identity of respondents by process of elimination. For instance, demographic reports for small work units could isolate and cast a spotlight on the responses of a female employee with fifteen years of service or of a male Pacific Islander. Report department or work unit results only when there are at least five respondents. Smaller groups' results can be reported along with the next biggest group.

Reports that show the responses to open-ended questions are called *comment reports*. Comment reports are even more sensitive. Word choice, spelling, and style can quickly reveal a respondent's identity. Comment reports should be presented only on a location-wide basis, not by department or work unit. Only summary comment reports should be presented for smaller units.

A difficult situation can arise when respondents use open-ended comments to level accusations anonymously toward another employee. It is best to decide at the start how such comments will be handled. The accusations may be true or false, but they must be handled very carefully. Under no circumstances should they be shared publicly. We recommend agreeing on a procedure for handling these before any cases arise. For instance, the policy might direct the damaging remarks to human resources, but not to immediate managers or senior management. If the procedure is outlined before these types of remarks occur, it is easier to deal with them.

Exhibit 7.1 lists some of the key points behind preservation of anonymity and confidentiality.

EXHIBIT 7.1

The Mechanics of Confidentiality

1. There is no good substitute for the use of a third party for data collection and report processing.

2. It is helpful to remind the location coordinators and managers to treat all employees as a group, not to single out employees by asking individuals if they have completed their questionnaires.

3. When using group meetings for survey administration, give employees the option to return surveys in prepaid return envelopes or to turn in their surveys in a sealed envelope in the meeting room.

4. When using group administration meetings, ask the last employee finished to seal the envelope or box containing all the surveys.

5. When using one-time passwords for Internet surveys, be sure to explain ahead of time why the password won't link the respondent with his or her responses.

6. Decide ahead of time how to handle accusations or other comments of a serious nature that identify individuals. Such accusations must be investigated according to the same investigation procedure that would be used with other human resource policy violations.

7. Announce ahead of time that no reports will be produced on groups of fewer than five responses.

How Should We Plan the Feedback Phase?

Feedback meetings are highly recommended. They are almost always done with large, all-employee surveys. Quick questionnaires may seem too short and focused to require feedback meetings. Perhaps a memo or a posting to the organization's intranet seems adequate.

We do not recommend on-line technology or other written communications as a first step in the feedback process, even for short, focused surveys. Anyone who was invited to complete the survey should be invited to learn the results firsthand. They can participate in live brainstorming. Written communications can play a significant role in the follow-up phase.

How Can We Win Support from Managers Whose Departments Are Included?

The first way to win support from managers is to involve them in the beginning of the process. This is one reason that employers often use steering teams.

A second key way to increase managers' comfort levels is to make a commitment ahead of time to a process called "trickle-up distribution." The key here is that department-level results go first to the department's manager. In large organizational surveys, such as annual all-employee surveys, the "front line" may be four or five steps removed from senior management. Senior managers may or may not review overall data before individual work units do. But the work unit supervisors and managers must always be the first to see results for their own units.

No survey, quick or otherwise, should ever become identified with a method of "finding the guilty." This will not only damage the outcome of the current survey but will create a negative atmosphere for future surveys.

With short, focused surveys such as the ones in this book and on the CD-ROM, the sponsoring manager may be only one or two levels from the work unit. The survey sponsor may be the manager of a small work unit. Senior management may never see the results from one of the quick questionnaires. The principle of trickle-up distribution still applies, but it is less complex. The front-line managers must have a chance to review data and, together with their departments, get a head start on action plans. When the next levels of management have a chance to review their results, front-line managers should be able to list some potential solutions. Prepared, they can answer questions fully.

In a full survey, we suggest the pattern of communications shown in Exhibit 7.2. The order shown encompasses all potential levels of involvement. Your distribution order may be much simpler. Adapt the idea as needed. In a short, focused survey, one or more of these steps may be eliminated.

EXHIBIT 7.2

Sample Order of Distribution of Survey Results

1. Senior management receives overall reports for the entire survey group. Reports are not presented by division, department, or work unit.

2. Division management receives division reports plus overall organization reports.

3. Senior management receives division reports after review by division management.

4. Department management receives department reports, plus overall and division reports.

5. Division management receives department reports after department management has reviewed them.

6. Senior management receives department reports after department and division management have reviewed them.

This trickle-up distribution is illustrated in the diagram:

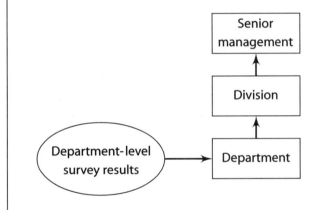

By communicating an order of distribution that ensures managers time to absorb their results, you will earn more trust and greater participation by managers.

What Should We Say in an Awareness Campaign?

An employee survey is not a command performance. Surveys can suffer from poor response rates, a factor that undermines confidence in the results. Therefore, most organizations have a presurvey communications plan.

The survey sponsor may need to "sell" employees on taking the survey at this stage, because its benefits may not be clear. Most potential respondents want to know, "What's in it for me?" Respondents also want to know their risk. They may wonder, "Is this survey safe and worth my time?" The sponsor must address these concerns in the course of making everyone aware of the upcoming survey.

The best presurvey communication answers questions such as these:

1. *Who is the sponsor?* It is important to select an effective sponsor. Respondents will be encouraged if they believe the person can make changes based on survey results.

2. *What is the purpose of the survey?* The goals, objectives, and a post-survey action plan need to be stated. Respondents want to know what useful outcome might occur.

3. *Who will see the results, and when?* Respondents must be told when they will see results, as well as who else will see results and when. This is usually where the concept of "trickle-up" distribution is introduced, as explained earlier in this chapter.

4. *Who designed and tested the questionnaire?* An explanation of how carefully the questionnaire was developed or selected can build credibility for the survey instrument itself.

5. *How will confidentiality and anonymity be addressed?* This is handled both by showing the safeguards that will be employed and by offering a promise that confidentiality will not be breached. For instance, in one awareness campaign letter, a senior manager wrote the following: "You may wonder why we ask so many questions about you, such as your location and length of employment. These are to help us produce reports that we will all find useful in understanding our workplace culture. We will not produce reports for any category where fewer than five responses are received. You have my promise that neither I nor the survey project team will relate responses to any one individual."

6. *How does the survey relate to broader initiatives?* The sponsor must explain how the survey relates to broader initiatives. A survey that is part of a well-publicized corporate initiative, such as a workplace of choice initiative, almost always gets higher response than one offered simply as a survey.

Awareness campaigns can incorporate many communications techniques, including posters, bulletin board announcements, drawings, and other attention-getting gimmicks. At the core of any such campaign, though, are three basic communications, usually carried out by e-mail:

1. Presurvey: Letter of introduction

2. Midsurvey: Reminder letter stating the cut-off date

3. Last minute: Final reminder

Of the three, the most important and complex is the initial letter of introduction.

Exhibits 7.3, 7.4, and 7.5 show three sample letters announcing a survey: one is for a large organization, another is for a small organization, and the third is in a question-and-answer format, which many organizations find appealing. Following these three sample letters, Exhibit 7.6 summarizes these key planning issues in a checklist.

• • •

In this chapter, you've learned the importance of making some survey decisions at the start. By selecting the survey team, identifying the right respondents, addressing anonymity and confidentiality, and designing a method for no-fault feedback, you're ready to answer the logical questions that respondents and their managers will raise. You can begin presurvey communications prepared to position the survey for success.

EXHIBIT 7.3

Sample Communications Survey
Awareness Letter for a Large Organization

From: Survey Sponsor

To: Associates of XYZ Division—Manufacturing Operations.

In the past six months, XYZ has made several changes in our organization. On March 4, you will receive a short employee survey that focuses on our communications under this new structure.

Why are we doing this survey? As our company grows, we need to ensure that communications are smooth between engineering, sales, and manufacturing. This is especially important as we increase staff size over the next several months.

All supervisors and employees in Manufacturing Operations will receive a letter explaining the survey results for their own department, for Manufacturing as a whole, and for the overall XYZ Division. You will have an opportunity to meet with your immediate department supervisors to review results and brainstorm action plans. Your suggested action plans will be shared with the Manufacturing Management Team at the quarterly management review. The team will see department results at that time, simultaneous with suggestions that are made at your survey review meetings.

All responses to this survey are confidential and anonymous.

We have asked you to identify your department, whether you are a manager, and your length of service with our company. We hope to see significant patterns in responses by particular groups so that issues can be locally addressed. A third-party survey firm is hosting the confidential survey on-line. This firm will not share raw data or summary reports that would reveal the identity of any individual respondents. It will not provide reports from work units where there are fewer than five responses. Furthermore, your department manager will share your department's results with you at a department meeting before they are submitted to the senior management team.

The survey has fourteen questions and provides an opportunity for you to enter two comments. It should take about 15 to 20 minutes to complete.

Please be sure to complete this survey between March 4 and March 11.

You may access the survey from home as long as you have a browser that is compatible with Internet Explorer (versions X and higher) or Netscape (versions X and higher).

Spanish-speaking respondents may take the Spanish version by checking "Espanol" on the opening screen.

Thank you for your support. Your opinions are most important to our continued progress.

Sincerely,

Survey Sponsor

EXHIBIT 7.4

Sample Morale Survey Awareness Letter for a Small, Fast-Growing Organization

Each of you plays an important part in our organization. Recent announcements about our plans to add significant numbers of employees have led to many questions. In order to understand the concerns and opinions of all employees, we are launching a thirty-question Morale Survey on our intranet. This survey will provide a benchmark about our readiness for significant change. It will help us to measure the success of our expansion efforts in future years.

This survey is your opportunity to express your views on a variety of issues. The survey should take no longer than 20 minutes to complete and will cover broad topics such as change readiness, overall satisfaction, and working conditions. The survey will be available for completion between August 24 and September 14. Please ensure that you take the time to provide your input.

The "team" with the highest percentage of completed surveys as of September 14 will receive their choice of an OUR COMPANY ball cap or T-shirt for each team member. "Teams" are established by the demographic information at the end of the survey. The earliest date of completion will be used to determine a tie.

Employees in any office who do not have Internet access at their desks can use the computer at either the help desk or in the library. When using these workstations, please log in with username: employee and password: Internet.

To complete the survey:

1. Access http://www.organizationsurvey.com/.

2. At the Company Code prompt, enter [code number].

3. At the survey ID prompt, enter [code number].

4. After reviewing the introduction page, select Continue.

5. Complete the survey by clicking on the bubble or drop-down list that best represents your answer, and type in the open question areas.

6. Click on the completed box to submit your survey.

Data are sent to a third-party survey firm. The data will be held in strictest confidence by our survey vendor. Your survey cannot be associated with you personally. Furthermore, all survey data will be aggregated into groups of at least five responses so that no individual responses can be identified in reports.

If you experience any technical difficulties, please contact the help desk for support. Your thoughts are important to us. By taking ownership and giving us your honest feedback, you will assist us in ensuring that together we meet our objectives. Reports for your department will go first to your department manager, who will share them with you in a department meeting before they are reviewed by the senior staff. You will have the opportunity to react, respond, and brainstorm for solutions at that time.

Regards,

Survey Sponsor

EXHIBIT 7.5

Announcement Letter in Question-and-Answer Format

Questions and Answers About Our Organization's Employee Engagement Survey

Why are we doing this survey? As part of our Workplace of Choice initiative, we need to ensure we make the right changes in our work environment so that we can keep growing. The purpose of this employee survey is to identify workplace issues that affect your commitment to the mission, goals, and plans of our organization.

Who designed the survey? An outside company specializing in this work designed the survey. The final questionnaire came as a result of meetings with several representative employee groups on [date]. The groups were asked to identify workplace issues that should be addressed by the survey. They also reviewed and completed draft questionnaires before the survey was finalized.

What happens after we answer? Employees will have an opportunity to meet with their managers to review survey results and discuss ways to make this an even better place for everybody to work. Your ideas will be forwarded to the administration executives along with department results. The executive team will not see any departmental reports before the departments have a chance to review and react to them.

Will my answers be identified? All responses to this survey are confidential and anonymous. An outside survey provider is collecting the data. It will not provide results or data for units in which there are fewer than five responses.

If my answers aren't going to be identified, why do you ask so many questions about me? We have also asked you to provide information about yourself, including your department, whether you are a manager, and your length of service with our company, etc. While these questions could potentially be used to identify you, you have my commitment that we will not do so. No one at our company will be given either raw data or summary reports that would allow any information to be reported for fewer than five individuals. Our intention in asking for this information from you is to see whether there are significant patterns in responses by particular groups.

How long is the survey? The survey has sixteen questions and an opportunity for you to respond to two open-ended comments. It should take no longer than about 15 minutes to complete.

When does the survey start? Please be sure to complete this survey between [date] and [date].

How do I access the survey? [Internet access instructions are included here.]

EXHIBIT 7.6

Presurvey Checklist

☐ Will you be able to share and act on the information you receive?

☐ Is the survey sponsor seen as the person most able to make a difference with the results?

☐ Have you designed a process for sharing the results?

☐ Who will see results first?

☐ How will respondent anonymity be protected?

☐ How will the data be kept confidential?

☐ What is the policy for investigating any accusations that arise?

Does the survey announcement letter:

☐ Explain why the survey is taking place?

☐ Recognize any difficulties or situations that motivated the decision to do a survey?

☐ Name the survey sponsor?

☐ Address anonymity?

☐ Address confidentiality?

☐ Relate the survey to broader goals and initiatives?

☐ Describe how the survey questions were selected?

☐ Describe a "no-fault" feedback process?

☐ Explain who will see the results and in what order they will receive them?

☐ Describe the administration process such as cut-off dates and method of data collection?

☐ Provide instructions for completing the survey?

Chapter 8

Customizing Your Questionnaire

WHAT'S IN THIS CHAPTER?

- Should We Get Employee Input About Questionnaire Topics?
- Can We Change Items in This Book?
- How Do We Write Our Own Questionnaire Items?
- How Many Questions Do We Need?
- What Types of Questions Should Be Included?
- Should We Pretest the Questionnaires?
- Can We Combine Items from Several of These Surveys?
- Can the Quick Questionnaires Be Combined to Create a Full-Length Employee Survey?
- Can We Add Open-Ended Questions to the Questionnaires?
- Can We Use a Different Response Scale?
- Should We Add Open-Ended Questions or Comments?
- What Demographics Should We Use?
- What About Multinational Questionnaires?

YOUR MANAGER ASKS you to write a quick questionnaire for a department where turnover has recently increased. You turn to our XYZ survey and find most of the topics covered, but you still need a few more items. What comes next?

Chapters Two, Four, Five, and Six provided a collection of twenty standard questionnaires. You may be wondering about adding some items of your own or customizing the ones found here. Better yet, you're wondering if you can put several quick questionnaires together and have a full-length questionnaire. This chapter addresses all these questions.

A big question for the survey sponsor is whether to develop your own survey items. In our opinion, there is a finite number of core questions that survey professionals, human resource professionals, and academics have already identified through years of trial and error. Nonetheless, the nuances of specific industries and individual businesses should be considered carefully in the creation of each survey.

You need to ask the right questions, and you must ask questions right. The average employee has to understand the intent of the question and feel encouraged to answer honestly. Asking questions is more difficult than it appears to be. The wording, length, and positioning of items can make a big difference in the results. This chapter offers some tips on using and enhancing the questionnaires in this book.

Should We Get Employee Input About Questionnaire Topics?

Employee input is almost always a good idea, even for short, focused surveys. Be aware, though, that employees may suggest topics that are uncomfortable for specific groups or individuals. Some questions can be difficult because they may result in negative feedback to specific groups. But the issues can be greatly increased when such a question is eliminated from a questionnaire after employee input showed that it was a desirable question. The sidebar "Difficult Questions" shows what happened when the senior executive at a medium-sized financial services firm deleted one such question.

Difficult Questions

The firm had done its homework well. It had solicited employee input through focus groups and had a thorough management review. But just before printing the surveys, a senior executive insisted on removing this questionnaire item:

I have trust and confidence in senior management.

He also decided that there should be no notification of the change to the employees who had been involved with the approval of what they thought was the final version. The surveys were printed without the bothersome question.

The firm was gathering data through group administration sessions over several days. During a session on the first day, one of the employees from the focus group asked the human resource manager where that particular question was. When he learned what had happened, the employee told others. This was a small enough firm that word spread quickly.

Attendance at later administration sessions dwindled. Employees did not respect the executive's decision and were disappointed they would not have the opportunity to answer the question. Those scheduled for sessions on the subsequent days were also more negative about their employment than those before news of the alteration got around.

Can We Change Items in This Book?

The CD-ROM that accompanies this book contains both PDF and Microsoft Word files for your use. The items, instructions, title, and demographics are all easily changed to suit your situation. The CD also contains a file with samples of demographics that you can copy and paste into your surveys. We show a sample of a customized survey in Exhibit 8.1.

EXHIBIT 8.1

Example of a Customized Quick Questionnaire

Employee Opinion Survey on the Individual Employee's Manager

INSTRUCTIONS

This survey was designed to get feedback from you regarding your work experiences with your manager at our organization. The results of this survey will enable our line managers to learn what they are doing well, as well as identify areas that may need improvement. Your responses will be completely anonymous. Survey results will be reported in general terms and will not identify individuals. Reports will show only the results of groups with five or more respondents. Managers will see their results first and then will hold department discussions on their feedback. This is being done in conjunction with XYZ's management training initiative.

All surveys will be collected by a professional survey vendor, and your individual responses will be held by them off-premises. **Please return your survey sealed in the envelope supplied to: ABC Survey Company, 20 Research Parkway, Anywhere, NY 00000, attn: XYZ Employee Survey. Return your survey by May 10 in order to have your opinions included.** Your feedback is greatly appreciated! Please be sure to use the following scale to define your response:

Strongly Disagree	Disagree	Neutral	Agree	Strongly Agree
1	2	3	4	5

1. My supervisor is fair in dealing with associates.   1 2 3 4 5
2. My supervisor ensures that associates who do a good job are recognized and appreciated.   1 2 3 4 5
3. My supervisor ensures that I am adequately informed about matters affecting me.   1 2 3 4 5
4. My supervisor gives me adequate feedback on the work I do.   1 2 3 4 5
5. My supervisor takes a supportive role in my growth and development.   1 2 3 4 5
6. My supervisor encourages me to do a good job.   1 2 3 4 5
7. My supervisor backs me when necessary.   1 2 3 4 5
8. I would feel comfortable going to my supervisor with a concern.   1 2 3 4 5
9. My supervisor helps me overcome problems in getting my work done.   1 2 3 4 5
10. My supervisor communicates well with everyone on the Blue Team.   1 2 3 4 5
11. My supervisor involves me in decisions that affect my work.   1 2 3 4 5
12. My supervisor gives me the freedom I need to do my job.   1 2 3 4 5
13. My supervisor provides the tools I need to do my job.   1 2 3 4 5

EXHIBIT 8.1

Example of a Customized Quick Questionnaire, Cont'd.

14. My supervisor sets clear goals and objectives.	1 2 3 4 5
15. It is clear how my supervisor will evaluate my performance.	1 2 3 4 5
16. My supervisor sets work objectives that motivate people.	1 2 3 4 5
17. My supervisor uses good judgment in making decisions.	1 2 3 4 5
18. My supervisor effectively coordinates the work flow among Blue Team members.	1 2 3 4 5
19. My supervisor makes decisions promptly when needed.	1 2 3 4 5
20. My supervisor is in control of what is going on in our department.	1 2 3 4 5
21. My supervisor tries to assign work to maximize productivity.	1 2 3 4 5

Please identify at least 2 or 3 suggestions for your supervisor:

Please identify at least 2 or 3 things that you feel your supervisor does well:

Thank you for your time and feedback!

Alterations

You can customize the quick questionnaire items without changing their meanings if you do not change the active portions of the statement: the verbs, adjectives, or objects of the action. If you do change these portions, you'll need to pretest the item. For instance, the following word change is safe and doesn't need to be pretested:

Standard item: This organization is a good place to work.

Customized item: Community Hospital is a good place to work.

In this example, the active portion of the statement stayed the same. It is essentially the same question. In the next example, the change creates a new meaning:

Standard item: This organization is a good place to work.

Customized item: Community Hospital provides a safe workplace.

The second item is about what the employer does, not the respondent's judgment about his or her place of work. Because the verb was changed, the value of the standard item is partially lost. It is now a new, untested item and must be pretested, a topic covered later in this chapter.

Customizing Instructions

The instructions section of each questionnaire is easily customized. You can add the name of a department or company, dates, the names of programs or initiatives that motivated the creation of a survey, or other items of interest. We strongly recommend adding an address where the survey can be sent. This will help facilitate responses.

How Do We Write Our Own Questionnaire Items?

Exhibit 8.2 offers some good practices and some to avoid. Exhibit 8.3 shows some actual survey items in the center column that we found on draft surveys written by clients. The problems with these statements are listed on the left column and the improved wording is shown in the right column. Using these pointers and examples will help in crafting your own statements.

To judge the viability of each question, ask yourself if it will pass the "use it" test. If employees answer unfavorably, will you be able to use their responses to do something? If not, reword the item or don't include it.

EXHIBIT 8.2

Best Practices in Questionnaire Development

	Good Practices	Practices to Avoid
Vocabulary selection	Keep it simple.	Avoid jargon unless you're certain the meaning is universally understood.
Sentence structure	Use one concept per question. A well-written question should imply a single action.	Avoid multiple concepts and compound sentences.
Sentence tone	Keep the wording positive.	Avoid negative words and phrases. Avoid double negatives.
Sentence length	Use short sentences and active voice.	Avoid long sentences and passive voice.
Spelling	Spelling must be impeccably correct.	Incorrect spelling can change meaning, aside from undermining the professional appearance of the survey.
Scale design[a]	Wherever possible, select a scale and stick with it for the entire survey.	If you must switch the meaning of the scales, never reverse the "negative" and "positive" aspects of a scale within the same survey. In other words, "1" should be the most negative choice on all scales, "5" the most positive.
	[a]A five-point scale, with 1 = Total disagreement, 5 = Total agreement, is highly recommended. Another good scale choice is "Very dissatisfied" to "Very satisfied."	Never use an even-numbered scale, such as 4 points or 6. This is a way to increase favorable results. Without the neutral category, people typically choose the more positive rating.
	If you are using different scales, group questions using the same scale together.	Avoid going back and forth, changing scales within a survey dimension.
Order of questions	Your first question should be the "overall" question. This helps gather the top-of-mind thoughts that form general opinions. This is called the respondent's "curb" opinion— what he or she would say if stopped on the sidewalk and asked the question without preparation. Keep related questions together on the page.	Never place controversial questions at the beginning.
Demographics	Place demographics, such as length of employment, at the end. People are more likely to answer once they know what they have said on the survey.	Placing demographics at the beginning can raise suspicions.
Number of questions per topic	Use three or four per topic. If you use three questions for one topic, keep the number consistent for all topics. It is good practice to keep related questions together on the survey page.	A common mistake is to "overquestion" one topic. This can give the employee an inaccurate perception of that topic's importance relative to the others. Also, if the questions aren't sufficiently different, they may be wasting precious space and time.

EXHIBIT 8.2

Best Practices in Questionnaire Development, Cont'd.

	Good Practices	Practices to Avoid
Selection of important topics	Let your early planning work with management and focus groups determine the most important topics.	Don't double the length of the survey by asking "how important" each item is to the respondent.
Context of questions and the use of customized questions for smaller respondent groups	For certain topics, you may need to customize questions so you can ask the people who are closest to the issue.	It is confusing, and even irritating, to be asked questions that are out of context or irrelevant.

Note: The *scale* is the rating selections that the survey offers respondents—for instance, 1 = Totally Disagree, 5 = Totally Agree.

EXHIBIT 8.3

Examples of Effective and Ineffective Wording

Sources of Error	Ineffective Wording	More Effective Wording
Negative wording	Training was inadequate to perform my job.	I received adequate training to perform my job.
Jargon and compound topics	OSHA and Baldrige practices are important to this organization.	1. Safety practices are important to this organization. 2. Quality practices are important to this organization.
Double-barreled question	I am satisfied with pay and the work environment.	1. I am satisfied with pay. 2. I am satisfied with the work environment.
Double negative	My manager does not do a bad job of keeping us informed.	My manager does a good job of keeping us informed.
Leading question	A good team player is committed to producing quality work.	1. People here are committed to producing quality work. 2. People here are good team players.
Passive voice	The people in this department are adequately informed by management's communications efforts.	Management's communications are effective.
Projecting the feelings of others	Customer service people in this organization feel well supported.	Customer service people are supported by the organization.
Misspelling	My coworkers' rolls are clear to me.	My coworkers' roles are clear to me.

How Many Questions Do We Need?

Employee surveys must ask a sufficient number of the right questions to assess the target issues. What is a sufficient number of questions? To increase your confidence in the results, you should ask three to four questions related to each topic. Consider this example on manager communications from the Employee Opinion Survey on the Individual Employee's Manager:

> *My manager ensures that I am adequately informed about matters affecting me.*
>
> *My manager gives me adequate feedback on the work I do.*
>
> *My manager communicates well with everyone in the department.*

Any one of these questions provides limited information. If a manager scores well on all three, it is a good indication of his or her skill as a communicator. Mathematically, the multiple questions on a single topic provide a more stable result.

That's one reason that short questionnaires, such as the ones in this book, should be focused on one or two topics. We have seen companies add single questions such as these on short questionnaires:

> *We recently launched a corporate ethics training program. If you have attended this program, how prepared do you feel to tackle the issues you may need to confront? [Scale = Not at All to Completely and a Not Applicable choice]*
>
> *Our elder-care benefits are adequate to meet your family's needs. [Scale = Strongly Disagree to Strongly Agree]*

In both cases, one or two more questions would add a great deal of information.

Still, a single question may be all that's required to get information on less searching topics—for example:

> *An adequate variety of our company's products is available at the company store. [Scale = Strongly Disagree to Strongly Agree]*

What Types of Questions Should Be Included?

Another issue related to the quantity of questions is the type of questions asked. We look at two types: judgmental and observational questions.

Two of the questions in the previous section lead to actions:

> *We recently launched a corporate ethics training program. If you have attended this program, how prepared do you feel to tackle the issues you*

*may need to confront? [Scale = Not at All to Completely and a Not
Applicable choice]*

*An adequate variety of our company's products is available at the
company store. [Scale = Strongly Disagree to Strongly Agree]*

In the first example, if people report feeling unprepared, the survey sponsor could conclude that additional preparation is needed. If company store
offerings are inadequate, more could be offered.

The third question asks for a broad judgment about the adequacy of a
program measured against the broad topic of a family's needs:

*Our elder-care benefits are adequate to meet your family's needs.
[Scale = Strongly Disagree to Strongly Agree]*

The first two are observational questions. The third is judgmental.

Most questions should be observational. Observational questions present
clear opportunities for action or at least invite more focused investigation. They
are also limited to one topic or variable. If the variable changes, a respondent's
level of agreement with the statement would presumably change. Therefore,
the survey giver could take action on that variable and improve opinion.

Judgmental questions, in contrast, ask for a personal judgment about a
broad topic. These questions can be problematic for the survey sponsor in that
they don't directly suggest what could be changed. Opinions on these broad
topics change slowly. Nonetheless, such questions are important because they
can offer a barometer against which to measure whether any action will be
sufficient to change negative opinions. Exhibit 8.4 gives some examples.

EXHIBIT 8.4

Comparison of Observational and Judgmental Questions

Sample Topics	Observational Questions	Judgmental Questions
Pay	I am paid fairly compared to what I could make elsewhere doing the same job.	I am paid fairly.
Management	Management communicates changes in a timely way.	Management communicates quickly enough to meet our needs.
My manager	My manager sets clear goals.	I am satisfied with goal setting by my manager.
Benefits	The benefits at this company are competitive with other companies in this region.	The benefits at this company meet my needs.

Consider the question of pay, the first example in Exhibit 8.4. Let's say a respondent agrees with the observation that he or she is paid fairly compared to what he or she would be paid elsewhere for the same job. If the questions ended here, we'd assume the respondent was satisfied. But what if the same respondent showed strong disagreement with the judgmental version of the question:

I am paid fairly.

In other words, this employee may feel that no one is paying fairly for employees' work. There may be little that a single employer could do to improve this judgment.

The majority of questionnaire items should be observational, but a few judgmental questions are an excellent way to get a general reading on opinions. They are also useful as the first questions in a survey. For instance, we open the Employee Opinion Survey on Employee Morale with the following statement:

Considering everything, I am satisfied working for this organization at the present time.

Such statements provide the summary judgment against which other observations can be judged. They can set the tone and ease the respondent into the observational questions.

Should We Pretest the Questionnaires?

If you write your own items or substantially alter ones in this book, you must pretest them with representatives of your survey population. This will help you detect if the question is understood as it was intended. One of the big dangers is differences in the perceived meanings of words.

A good pretest will increase your confidence that the language seems genuine to the different groups who will take the survey. For example, the following question was inserted in a teamwork survey: "I feel willing to cooperate with other departments." During the questionnaire pretest, customer service employees reacted poorly to the wording of this question. They felt it questioned their willingness to cooperate but ignored a bigger issue. They believed the organization's roles were unclear, making it difficult to know how to give or receive cooperation. The question was reworded as follows: "I know which department to call so I can give customers the best service." The final survey showed 40 percent of customer service personnel were confused about whom to call.

The meaning and weight of a word such as *safety,* for instance, can vary dramatically among a hospital, a construction firm, a transportation organization, and a computer-driven financial services firm. *Safety* can also have a different context within the same organization. Office workers in a relatively low-risk environment have a different relationship with the concept than do people in a manufacturing plant using toxic chemicals.

The case study in the sidebar, "Using the Word *Risk* Can Be Risky," provides a good example of what can go wrong when pretesting is inadequate. This also illustrates what can happen in multinational situations.

Using the Word *Risk* Can Be Risky

A large corporation with global manufacturing operations was conducting a worldwide employee survey. The U.S.-based corporate steering team, including several members of top management, drafted and finalized the survey. Although the corporate staff made up only 10 percent of the survey population, they pretested survey content only at corporate headquarters.

One item caused a stir:

I am encouraged to take risks. [Scale = Disagree to Agree]

In American business culture, risk taking has positive associations, almost on a par with noble causes. A businessperson in the United States who agreed with the statement would be saying something positive. At a manufacturing plant in Spain, where toxic materials are handled every day, respondents thought they were being asked whether they were being encouraged to place themselves in danger. A person who agreed would be making a very negative statement about his or her workplace.

An error of this sort has a big impact. First, an Agree response can have vastly different meaning depending on the source. This invalidates the responses to that question. For those who take the word *risk* negatively, its inclusion is at best confusing. It might also communicate a lack of sensitivity and understanding or reinforce bad feelings about the central staff. Elsewhere in the survey, items referred to a forty-hour workweek and "24/7 operations." These phrases have meaning only in certain circumstances.

The moral of the story is that pretesting is valuable any time, but it is crucial in multinational situations.

Here are some ideas for examining the questionnaire's readiness for publication:

- If focus groups were used during the planning phases, they can give their reactions to the draft survey.

- Invite review from representative members of the respondent groups to take a trial run by completing the draft questionnaires. Then have them report reactions and difficulties they may have encountered.

- Read the entire questionnaire aloud to yourself or a listener. Awkward sentences, jargon, and other wording problems often reveal themselves in this way.

Each of these examples is persuasive of the fact that pretesting is key to the success of any survey, particularly if it is customized.

Can We Combine Items from Several of These Surveys?

This can be done, but to cover a topic adequately, three to four questionnaire items should be used. Remember to add enough items. A score derived from multiple items is more consistent than scores derived from one. If you are targeting too many topics, the questionnaire may become broader than you intended for a short, focused survey.

Can the Quick Questionnaires Be Combined to Create a Full-Length Employee Survey?

The questionnaires in this book are not designed as cut-and-paste modules, but they might be a starting point for a full-length questionnaire. Check for repetition, because the quick questionnaires share some of the same questions. Also, the order of questions is important. Generally, start with an overall opinion question. If you have any sensitive questions, leave them for later in the order. Finally, a questionnaire created this way must be pretested.

Can We Add Open-Ended Questions to the Questionnaires?

The CD-ROM versions of the questionnaires that accompany this book all have sample open-ended questions. These can be used or new ones can be substituted.

Can We Use a Different Response Scale?

We use a five-point Likert scale (Exhibit 8.5), the most common scale in attitudinal research. A five-point scale is widely considered to represent the "natural" number of opinion plateaus or levels. Note that all questionnaire items in this book are to be answered on this scale. We do not recommend changing this, especially for the items in the Employee Opinion Survey on Employee Morale. Changing the scale would invalidate the norms provided in that chapter.

EXHIBIT 8.5

Five-Point Likert Agreement Scale

Strongly Disagree	Disagree	Neutral	Agree	Strongly Agree
1	2	3	4	5

Should We Add Open-Ended Questions or Comments?

In our experience, all surveys are improved by open-ended comments. The opportunity to provide comments is valued by respondents, who can explain why a rating was or was not given and add what's important to them. Open-ended questions tell employees that you're not trying to fit their thoughts into a numerical format alone. In addition, individuals may include suggestions or ideas that would make a positive difference in the organization. Usually three or fewer comment-type questions are included in a survey.

Typical open-ended questions include the following:

Please identify at least 2 or 3 things that we should be doing to improve as an organization.

Please identify at least 2 or 3 things that you like about working for this organization.

As the interpreter of the comments, remember that they are individual statements. Don't give excessive weight to any single comment or handful of comments. Look for them to validate the broader numerical results.

What Demographics Should We Use?

The CD-ROM accompanying this book has samples of demographic elements that can be easily added to the electronic versions of the questionnaires. Length of employment, location, and level are all useful. These are invaluable in creating reports, describing trends, and spotting problems. You should use whatever demographics will help you identify problem areas *as long as they are not used to identify individuals.* We covered this topic in Chapter Seven, but it is worth noting again. Demographics sometimes raise concerns about anonymity, particularly in smaller groups. To some extent, communicating your intentions to report on cells with only five or more responses can allay this concern.

We recommend placing demographic questions at the end of a survey. A person who has finished the questionnaire and feels comfortable with its tone and content will perceive less risk in answering the demographic questions. A person who encounters a demographics section before looking at a single question will have none of this comfort. Some sample demographic elements are shown in Exhibit 8.6.

EXHIBIT 8.6

Examples of Demographic Elements

Department demographic for use with a small number of departments

76. **DEPARTMENT:**
- ○ Accounting
- ○ Human Resources
- ○ Manufacturing
- ○ R&D
- ○ Technology

The following method of collecting demographics works when there are many choices. It is accompanied by a list of answer codes.

A. Use only the questions and/or codes provided on the insert to answer the following questions.	Example:	0	5

1. What is your **position** in the organization?

2. Which **department** do you work for the greatest portion of your time?

3. To which **unit** do you report or primarily support?

Example Department Key:
Engineering = 01
Marketing = 02

Example Position Key:
Associate = 10
Manager = 11

6.

For analysis purposes only, please indicate the country or Global Group you belong to:

- ○ Argentina
- ○ Australia
- ○ Canada
- ○ Honduras
- ○ Hong Kong
- ○ India
- ○ Indonesia
- ○ Ireland
- ○ Philippines
- ○ Poland
- ○ Portugal
- ○ Russia
- ○ South Africa
- ○ Spain
- ○ United States
- ○ Global Marketing
- ○ Other:_____

7.

Please indicate to which function you belong.

(choose only one)
- ○ 1. General management
- ○ 2. Finance
- ○ 3. Marketing
- ○ 4. Operations or Customer service
- ○ 5. MIS or ITS
- ○ 6. Other:_____

Employee Opinion Questionnaires. Copyright © 2005 by John Wiley & Sons, Inc. Reproduced by permission of Pfeiffer, an Imprint of Wiley. www.pfeiffer.com

EXHIBIT 8.6

Examples of Demographic Elements, Cont'd.

About Yourself:

Please answer the following questions about yourself. We will use this information to analyze survey responses in various ways. UNDER NO CIRCUMSTANCES WILL WE PRODUCE A REPORT OR PROVIDE DATA THAT RESULTS IN FEWER THAN FIVE RESPONDENTS IN A CATEGORY. Reports or data will not be provided to our company that would allow anyone to identify any individual's answers to any survey questions.

Please check the circle that best describes you:

Sample Locations:
- ○ New York, NY
- ○ Tucson, AZ
- ○ Seattle, WA
- ○ Denver, CO
- ○ Boston, MA
- ○ San Diego, CA

Sample Department:
- ○ Accounting
- ○ HR
- ○ Manufacturing
- ○ Technology
- ○ R&D
- ○ Advertising

Sample Work Schedule Classification:
- ○ Temporary
- ○ Part time
- ○ Full time
- ○ On call

Sample Tenure:
- ○ Less than 1 year
- ○ 1 to 3 years
- ○ 4 to 6 years
- ○ 7 years or more

Sample Job Classification:
- ○ Exempt
- ○ Nonexempt

Sample Level Classification:
- ○ Support Staff
- ○ Individual Contributor
- ○ Supervisor
- ○ Manager
- ○ Director
- ○ Vice President

What About Multinational Questionnaires?

The advice and surveys presented in this book are useful for multinational audiences. We have used much of the material and have performed many of our surveys in more than thirty-five countries. Nevertheless, it is important to consider the issues in conducting a multinational survey.

If you wish to use the material in this book for non-English-speaking populations or even for non-U.S. English-speaking cultures, it is less important that the item be translated literally and more important that the same basic meaning be suggested. At the item level, avoid jargon and keep questions short and direct. Our earlier comments about sensitivity to the context need to be repeated here. Just as words like *safety, support, trust,* and *communications* can have different meanings within an organization of the same language and culture, the effect can be magnified across multiple languages and cultures. (Most of the questions in this book have been used in translation.)

The procedure we follow is to write questions so they are "translation ready," that is, avoiding any known troubles with words and concepts. Certain phrases go through waves of popularity in every culture. A recent one in U.S. business is "walking the talk." One might be tempted to ask a question such as this:

Management in this organization "walks the talk"; they do as they say.

This item is most emphatically not translation ready! Now consider this statement:

Management in this organization acts consistently; they do as they say.

Here, we lose something in the original language by having to abandon the popular phrase, but we gain better communications with a diverse audience.

Items should be translated from the writer's language by one person and translated back into the original language by a second translator. The target language should be the translator's native language. Sometimes the retranslations are surprising. We often revise the English version at this point to reflect a more universal rendition. The only impediments to translating a survey are the expense and time involved in doing it well.

Some local questions can strengthen the survey in multinational situations. This gives a friendlier tone to the questionnaire and communicates that the survey giver is respecting local issues. It will be better accepted—and therefore more effective—when working cross-culturally. Endeavor to keep the demographics consistent across locations, however, so that reports can show survey results for each item across all the languages and cultures involved.

•   •   •

Typically, the quick questionnaires provide you with sufficient material. But if they do not, this chapter has covered some of the important issues of questionnaire development. Customization may increase your survey's success.

Chapter 9

Report Preparation and Data Interpretation

WHAT'S IN THIS CHAPTER?

- What Are Standard Elements of an Employee Survey Report?
- How Do We Set Standards for Interpretation?
- How Should We Interpret Neutral Ratings?
- What Are Some Approaches to Reviewing the Data?
- What Are Some Approaches to Reviewing the Comments?
- What Are the Rules of Rounding?
- What Software Features Are Required to Produce Reports?

ONCE RESULTS ARE processed, most people ask the same questions: "What do the data really tell us? When is a result unacceptably negative? At what level do I know I have a positive strength?" They are also concerned with how to present the data. This chapter offers tips on how to approach those questions.

What Are Standard Elements of an Employee Survey Report?

There are several approaches to writing a report, and each should leave the reader with an understanding of both the strengths and the issues of key concern. A typical report contains the following sections:

1. Overview and survey objectives
2. Key observations
3. Purpose of survey

4. Profile of participants (number surveyed, number in various demographic groups)

5. Results by scale (ranked from most to least favorable)

6. Listing of the most favorable survey items (see Exhibit 9.1)

7. Listing of the most unfavorable survey items (see Exhibit 9.2)

8. Item-by-item results showing percentages (with bar charts; the horizontal bar chart is an easy-to-read and well-accepted format widely used for reporting "favorable," "neutral," and "unfavorable" results on employee surveys; see Exhibit 9.3)

9. Additional analysis, such as comparisons with norms or with past surveys (see Exhibit 9.4)

EXHIBIT 9.1

Example of Most Favorable Survey Items

The overall results reflect the opinions of $N = 2,550$ respondents.

Item Number		Unfavorable	Neutral	Favorable
Q2	Employees consider this a very good place to work.	5%	20%	75%
Q6	The people I work with care a great deal about the quality of their work.	12	15	73
Q10	Employees in my organization generally trust one another and offer support.	3	6	71

EXHIBIT 9.2

Example of Least Favorable Survey Items

Overall results reflect the opinions of $N = 2,550$ respondents.

Item Number		Unfavorable	Neutral	Favorable
Q8	I receive the information I need about changes that affect my work.	55%	20%	25%
Q11	Information is communicated in a timely manner.	53	35	12
Q14	Information is communicated openly and honestly at this organization.	51	26	23

EXHIBIT 9.3

Overall Company Report

Reading Your Results

This report was designed to summarize the opinions given by individuals regarding the job and work environment at your organization. The information below describes how to read the results.

"Perspective" refers to the group of employees rating each question.

"Actual" refers to the actual number of individuals who responded to a particular question.

"NR" refers to the number of employees who left the item blank.

"% of Responses" refers to the percentage of "Actuals" who responded with a 1, 2, 3, 4, or 5. Due to rounding, the totals of these percentages may be slightly above or below 100%.

"SD" refers to the standard deviation. SDs greater than 1.0 indicate a relatively high level of disagreement and should be examined more closely.

"AVG" refers to the average. This is the average of all responses for a particular question.

Bar charts are based on the following scale:
  1 = Strongly Disagree
  2 = Disagree
  3 = Neutral
  4 = Agree
  5 = Strongly Agree

The actual results from question 1 are given below as an example:

---

1. Overall, I am satisfied working for this organization at the present time.

			% of Responses							Unfavorable – Favorable		
Perspective	Actual	NR	1	2	3	4	5	SD	AVG			
Our Organization	2,250	14	2	8	21	51	18	0.9	3.74	10	21	69

NOTE: Ratings are indicated as a percentage value and graphically represented by a bar chart.

Unfavorable ratings (1s and 2s) are shown as a percentage and represented as a black bar on the accompanying chart.

Neutral ratings (3s) are shown as a percentage and represented as a white bar on the accompanying chart.

Favorable ratings (4s and 5s) are shown as a percentage and represented as a gray bar on the accompanying chart.

Depending on the actual results, there may be any combination of these three bars on your reports. The longest bar represents the predominant view of each group. Due to rounding, the combined percentages of these three bars may be slightly above or below 100%.

EXHIBIT 9.4

**Example of Additional Analysis:
Company Comparison with General Industry Norms**

	Our Organization	General Industry Norm
Satisfied	71%	59%
Neutral or undecided	15	25
Dissatisfied	16	14

How Do We Set Standards for Interpretation?

Standards are the cutoff points at which you describe a result as acceptable or unacceptable and therefore an item for further discussion and investigation. There are a number of ways to set standards. We recommend choosing only one of them, but here are five to consider.

Absolute Standard

This is the most common approach: the results are compared to some general percentage ranges. Generally ratings of at least 67 percent, or about two out of three favorable responses, indicate a strength or positive result. It is important to note that when sample sizes are small, one individual's ratings can have an impact. However, two out of three favorable responses still mean there was one response that was either neutral or unfavorable. In other words, there is still opportunity for improvement.

Here is a typical "absolute" standard:

Dissatisfaction:

35 percent or more—Critical

20 to 34 percent—Danger

10 to 20 percent—Pay attention

0 to 10 percent—Probably unavoidable dissatisfaction on any issue, but low enough that you need not be too concerned

Satisfaction:

75 percent or more—Outstanding strength

67 to 74 percent—Strength

Below 67 percent—Watch the neutral and negative zones, potential danger for an area of high dissatisfaction

Comparative Standard

Do you have a basis for comparison, such as a prior survey administration? Compare percentages between your organizational unit, department, or location, for example, and the organization overall. Is your unit different? A difference of more than 5 to 10 percent, depending on the total population, may be important.

Personal Standard

Are your results less favorable than you would like them to be? Some managers may focus on areas important to them. For example, some may consider 80 percent satisfaction with communications excellent. Some may feel anything less than 90 percent is unacceptable.

External Standard

Compare the results to those from other organizations, such as other industry members or other employers in your region. How do the results for your work group compare with those of the wider world? An internal perceived weakness sometimes looks like a strength when taken in a larger perspective, or vice versa. For example, you may find low satisfaction with salary levels in your unit relative to the overall organization. But perhaps both your unit and your organization look pretty good when compared to external norm groups.

"Reasonable Person" Standard

Sometimes it is helpful to think of the expectations the audience will apply. What would a reasonable person in the audience expect for positive, neutral, and negative responses?

How Should We Interpret Neutral Ratings?

Neutral ratings are very important but somewhat difficult to interpret. For instance, if one-third of respondents or more are neutral on an item, it may signal an unimportant item or something that is not an issue. It may also mark an area in transition to more positive or negative responses. If neutral ratings are more than 50 percent, the item itself may be a problem. Rewording may improve its ability to detect opinions. The point would be to improve the response by giving respondents more clearly worded alternatives.

If the survey is repeated, pay attention to items that previously had high neutral ratings for changes.

What Are Some Approaches to Reviewing the Data?

One possibility is to scan through survey results a few times before making any conclusions. The first time, look through overall reports to identify the most favorable and unfavorable results. As you revisit the data, focus on patterns of results, including apparent inconsistencies. In the example that follows, the "immediate manager" question rated positively, while "management in general" was less positive. The combined information is far more powerful than either items alone:

I am supported by my immediate manager.

Strongly Agree	*15 percent*
Agree	*55 percent*
Total Favorable	*70 percent*

Senior management supports the employees of this organization.

Strongly Agree	*4 percent*
Agree	*20 percent*
Total Favorable	*24 percent*

This may be a case where one or two senior managers are seen negatively, causing all employees to feel that they and their managers support one another against a larger force. This then becomes an interesting opportunity for intervention.

Another approach is to compare percentages among demographic groups, such as length of employment, location, job classification, and professional status, to find the places where satisfaction and dissatisfaction are the greatest. Is one group different? How do the subgroups compare with the organization overall? A difference of more than 5 to 10 percent may be significant.

Use the standard deviation to determine how much confidence you should have in a result. (Another name for standard deviation is the *disagreement index,* a term considered to be more user friendly.) It shows the spread of the ratings or the degree of disagreement among the raters.

Standard deviations in small groups can be very large. This is because when there are only, say, five responses, the ratings of one individual have a lot of impact. If one is highly negative (or positive), the average will be affected more than might have been the case in a larger group. On a daily basis, a small group is probably affected in the same way if the group is made up of coworkers. But the percentages may not be easy to extrapolate to the larger group.

What Are Some Approaches to Reviewing the Comments?

Comments should be reviewed before general publication. This will help you categorize them into positive and negative summaries. Most companies edit them for misspellings and poor grammar. In addition, expletives are generally removed. Ideally, comments should also be reviewed for the following:

- Lack of anonymity. Did a person inadvertently identify himself or herself through comments?

- Damaging remarks about individuals. As discussed in Chapter Seven, people sometimes use the open-ended comments to deliver accusations anonymously. We recommend having a plan for dealing with this issue before it arises. Most employers have a policy for investigating possible infractions. It should be used in this situation.

- Intended meaning. If you are classifying comments into "positive" and "negative" categories, several people may have to sort them. Since comments are written extemporaneously, their intention may be unclear. It will be helpful to have several opinions.

Yet another approach is to compare written comments to trends in the numerical responses. Comments help employees expand on ratings they gave during the survey. They provide participants the opportunity to explain why a rating was or was not given and to address areas that are not covered in the survey yet are still considered important.

Avoid using comments, though, to summarize the message of the survey. Comments should be used only to illustrate the story told by the numbers. Avoid individual written comments to prove a point, and don't overweight issues with a few inflammatory or pithy remarks. If you want to group them, it is best to keep the groupings general, such as positive and negative comments. Look for the open-ended comments to confirm the numerical results.

What Are the Rules of Rounding?

Rounding errors can stop a meeting and cause the feedback leader to spend time explaining the error. To avoid this, follow the rules for rounding:

Rule 1

In determining a percentage, use the actual number of people who give a particular rating, such as 5 for Strongly Agree. Divide by the total number of respondents who answered the question. To illustrate this, think of a survey where 29 people responded Strongly Agree (a score of 5) to a question out of 245 people who answered it in total. The percentage of people who respond with Strongly Agree would be 29/245 = 0.1183. Multiplying this by 100 percent, you get 11.83 percent.

Rule 2

Round up if the digit following the decimal is 0.5 or higher. Round down if the digit following is 0.4 or lower. In the previous example, round 11.83 percent to 12 percent.

Rule 3

Always round any calculation once—do not perform further calculations on rounded numbers. To reduce potential distortion in rounding, we always round once on a base number. The alternative of using rounded numbers in further calculations can quickly result in severe distortion of data when samples are small and response ranges limited (as is almost always the case with employee survey data). In the second illustration, 97 people out of 245 rated the same question mentioned above Agree. This results in 39.59 percent, which rounds to 40 percent.

The rounded percentages add to 52 percent. But if we use the actual numbers to obtain the percentage of all people responding favorably, we get 51.42 percent. This rounds to 51 percent. Because of rounding, Percentage Favorable to Percentage Unfavorable distributions can range from 98 to 102 percent. These rounding errors can lead to useless and distracting discussion during employee feedback meetings, so be prepared to explain your rounding rules.

What Software Features Are Required to Produce Reports?

The software vehicle must be robust enough to provide cross-tabs, statistics, graphics, and text. There are a number of resources on the Web, as well as software products, to run on in-house servers with database and reporting capabilities built in. If you are using paper, you will need to select software for processing and reporting.

It is beyond the scope of this book to examine all of the many available survey products. However, here are some features to consider in your search:

- Text and data. Does the database allow you to prepare textual, numeric, and graphical information? Some readers prefer numerical tables and others graphs, so providing both in the same report is desirable.

- File size. Does the database produce reasonably sized reports? Some simple databases create "one-page per item" types of reports that get very cumbersome very fast.

- Export capabilities. Does the database allow you to export to other software products, such as Microsoft Access, Microsoft Excel, SPSS, and various human resource information systems?

- Anonymity. Does the database enable the anonymity promised to respondents? For instance, will it suppress results that have fewer than five respondents? How does the password feature work? Are data protected from other users and unauthorized use by the software vendor?

- Flexibility. Are report formats flexible? Inevitably, someone will ask for a format change. Can reports be modified and the data easily rerun? In case of late survey responses, you want to be able to produce updated reports without extra set-up time. Can the reports be produced in real time for previews and trial versions?

- Color. Can the report be provided in color? Color reports are easier and quicker to interpret and are more thoroughly read than black and white. Color is highly recommended.

- Multiple languages. Can the reports be presented in multiple languages?

- Norms. Can the product present normative data with your survey data?

Chapter 10

Feedback and Action Planning

WHAT'S IN THIS CHAPTER?

- How Should Feedback Meetings Be Structured?

- What Are Some Tips for Surviving the Dynamics of Feedback Meetings?

- What Happens When Difficult Situations Arise?

- What Are Some Tips for Action Planning?

PROVIDING SURVEY feedback to a group of employees can be challenging. This is especially the case for managers who are surprised by their own department's results. Often they are receiving feedback on their performance. This chapter offers some tips on the feedback portion of the survey process.

How Should Feedback Meetings Be Structured?

The meeting should be structured to both give and get information. In larger surveys, typically two or more meetings are held. The first meeting is primarily for dissemination of information and the follow-up meetings for action planning. Shorter questionnaires may not require multiple meetings, but brainstorming for actions should certainly be part of the process. Exhibit 10.1 shows an employee survey feedback meeting agenda. Exhibit 10.2 shows an action planning meeting agenda. You may want to combine them for shorter surveys.

EXHIBIT 10.1

Sample Agenda for Employee Feedback Meeting

1. Review survey purpose, format, and administration.

2. Review survey response rate.

3. Distribute results; provide time for reading.

4. Review results.

5. Manager's interpretation of results.

6. Conduct initial feedback session for reactions to manager's interpretation and suggested action plans.

7. Schedule follow-up meetings to determine progress on action plans from step 6 and to develop more action plans.

8. Schedule action planning meetings.

Employee Opinion Questionnaires. Copyright © 2005 by John Wiley & Sons, Inc. Reproduced by permission of Pfeiffer, an Imprint of Wiley. www.pfeiffer.com

---

EXHIBIT 10.2

Sample Agenda for Action Planning Meeting

1. Review the survey outcome briefly.

2. Ask the group to select the two or three most important results, one of each type listed below.

3. Ask the group for ideas on possible actions and solutions in key areas for improvement for each area. Develop initial action plans for each of these issues.

4. Identify areas that can be acted on at this level and must be addressed at higher levels.

5. Record action plans for consensus.

6. Develop dates, responsibilities, and milestones.

Employee Opinion Questionnaires. Copyright © 2005 by John Wiley & Sons, Inc. Reproduced by permission of Pfeiffer, an Imprint of Wiley. www.pfeiffer.com

What Are Some Tips for Surviving the Dynamics of Feedback Meetings?

Feedback meetings are dynamic situations in which challenging opinions may be aired and difficult situations may arise. We offer the following tips for handling them:

Prepare Adequately

Feedback meeting leaders must be willing and able to address any question about the survey or its results, and without defensiveness. The feedback meeting leader has enormous impact on the acceptance of the data and ensuing action plans. If the leader is unprepared or unwilling to address challenges and questions, survey results are more likely to be rejected.

Provide Sufficient Time for Feedback Meetings

Short questionnaires can often be handled in one-hour meetings. A full-length survey of fifty to one hundred questions usually requires a two-hour initial session. Additional sessions are often scheduled for action planning and progress reports.

Keep Meetings Small

Try to keep the number or participants under twenty employees. These meetings are being held to maximize communications, so the smaller the better.

Set an Agenda at the Beginning of the Meeting

Make it clear that two or three specific issues will be identified for further action. Two issues are ideal, one of them a department issue that can be addressed by the people in the meeting.

State a Goal to Develop Specific Action Plans

Typically, it is best to identify only two or at most three action plans. One or two of them should be items that can be handled by the people in the meeting. The other one or two should be passed to upper management for action.

Agree on progress measurements during the meeting, and include responsibilities and dates. Departments need to set up a measurement for achievement of action plans. Exhibit 10.3 shows a feedback meeting action plan worksheet. Exhibit 10.4 shows the contents of an actual follow-up worksheet.

Describe Follow-Up Plans

Make it clear that follow-up meetings or on-line discussions will take place to learn whether the problems are being addressed. (See the section titled "What Are Some Tips for Action Planning?" on page 146.)

EXHIBIT 10.3

Survey Action Follow-Up

WORK GROUP: DATE:

Information provided by:
(one-sentence summary description)

Action taken to date:

Issue/action plan considered complete? Yes _____ No _____

If not, please indicate open action items or issues:

Target completion date: _____

EXHIBIT 10.4

Sample Survey Feedback Action Plan for a Software Engineering Department

Organizational Unit	Information Provided by	Action Item	Action Taken to Date	Issue/Action Complete?
Software Engineering	S. Jones J. Smith	1. Manager communicates well with everyone in the department—42% disagreement	1. Request all staff to install new interoffice communications software. Provide training where necessary.	Yes; 6/30
		2. Needs to inform personnel on scheduled availability	2. Create calendar of staff events on department calendar	Yes; 7/10
		3. Needs to spend more time with junior personnel	3a. Modify agenda of one-on-one meetings, when requested. Include demos, presentations, and seminar materials for personnel with less than two years' tenure.	In process
			3b. Draft a protocol guide for Software Engineering—distribute for informal sign-off.	
		4. Needs to be clear about roles.	4. Draft guide detailing roles/responsibilities of function vs. project management. Distribute for sign-off.	In process

Sandwich Sensitive or Controversial Results

Insert the unfavorable news inside more favorable results so you leave employees on a positive note. For example, consider this sequence:

1. Introduction

2. Favorable results

3. Unfavorable results

4. Sensitive subjects

5. A favorable concluding result

6. Summary and discussion of next steps

Don't Shy Away from Controversial or Embarrassing Results

If a manager is surprised by his or her results, provide sufficient time for this person to face reality and develop a way to converse about the feedback. Otherwise, employees might misread this as an intent to "cover up" results, undermining all the work done to produce positive commitment. Some managers may need support and rehearsal, but don't dodge the hard issues.

What Happens When Difficult Situations Arise?

In our experience, most feedback meetings are positive experiences. Occasionally, though, difficult situations can arise. The feedback leader's handling of them can have a lot of impact on the ultimate success of action plans. Therefore, it is important to prepare for the many reactions people can have. The following list covers some we have seen.

One Employee Dominates the Meeting

Domination by one or a few people is the biggest single threat to a positive, problem-solving atmosphere. These vocal employees may have good points, but they may also make it difficult for others to join in. The meeting leader owes it to all attendees to balance these individuals' comments with opportunities for others.

One method for reducing the impact of dominant participants is to redirect the conversation. The speaker may ask a simple question of a more moderate member of the audience and then ask for reactions from others. Invariably some will agree, and others will not. Get all views out on the table to round out the discussion—for example, "I think I understand your point on this, Bill. What do the rest of you think about this topic? Have I underestimated how important it is to the rest of you?"

Another method is to anticipate who the more vocal employees may be and give them a role in the meeting. For instance, they might become the facilitators for brainstorming or the keepers of the action recommendations.

People Disbelieve or Deny Results

Audience members may reject the survey process, questioning its sincerity or honesty. Just as managers might be shocked or try to deny results, employees may be incredulous at a result. Perhaps they don't feel their views are adequately represented. Perhaps they suspect the data have been altered.

In this situation, avoid subtle or direct retorts, put-downs, or jokes made at the speaker's expense. This situation calls for a direct, confident response. One temptation under these circumstances is to respond to the critic's negativity, particularly if it's a person who is chronically negative.

One method of handling this is to focus on the problem, not the messenger: "I can understand that you have questions about how the data were gathered and what they mean. Let's review the process and try to answer any questions you have about how the data was handled." Here are some other tips:

- *Insist on specifics:* As you review results from particular questionnaire items, general criticisms might come out—for instance, "If they would just fix the order entry system around here . . . " or "If someone would remember to communicate with us, XYZ wouldn't keep happening." Ask for specific details. What about the order entry system isn't working? When do communications need to occur?

- *Turn the complaint into an opportunity to solicit other opinions:* As you review results from particular questionnaire items, negative comments may arise such as, "Management is always promising action and then doesn't come through," or "Nobody ever gets recognized in this organization." Publicly, you might say, "Okay, I think we have a clear idea of one perspective here. Are there other perspectives we need to consider at the same time?" You might also say privately to the individual, "Can you give me an example of a time when you felt overlooked for a contribution you made?" If your inquiry is sincere, you may get useful information.

- *Turn the complaint into a call for positive action:* "I think we have a few people who feel this is a big problem. Who has an idea on how we might improve?"

People Express Discouragement or Pessimism

Nonmanagement workers often feel a lack of control over their work: "Nothing makes a difference here." If a negative atmosphere has been present for a while, they may come to the meetings very discouraged or cynical. They will not be effective participants in the solution until this is recognized.

One method of handling this is to summarize the complaint: "You feel that absolutely nothing can be done to address this situation." The person may respond, "That's right," or may take this as an opening to become more specific.

If you believe that others in the audience have more tolerant or moderate views, you might ask, "Does anyone else have a different perspective or have any suggestions to offer?" If other viewpoints emerge, it will help to balance the atmosphere of the meeting.

Audience Members Are Afraid to React Honestly

In some environments, people will disguise their reactions. They may fear retaliation, either subtle or direct. Disguised reactions are not helpful to the process. This is another good reason that honesty and sincerity must be built into the entire process.

One method of addressing this situation is to start with simple topics and ask questions that can be answered with yes or no. This may cause people to relax and become more talkative. If you believe before the meeting that this is an issue that will come up, be prepared with a list of simple questions to get the conversation started.

Audience Members Blame Others

Employees or work units may feel that all their problems originate elsewhere. The feedback meeting speaker must be prepared for this. He or she should practice the art of turning questions and comments around in such a way to induce people to accept responsibility for what they can do.

One method is to use the Rule of Two: feedback groups brainstorm for solutions, then narrow their focus to two items that will be assigned. One of the items is something the group can address itself. The other will be handed off to someone outside the group, such as the next level of management. Exhibit 10.3 provides a worksheet for recording action plans.

People Won't Participate

Some people may visibly refuse to join in, taking a passive-aggressive stance. Others may feel dominated by louder voices or may be afraid of speaking in front of other audience members.

One method of responding is to direct simple yes or no questions to these individuals. This may help them relax and can create an opening to engage them in more participation.

•   •   •

Although it's important to expect the difficult moments, in our experience most feedback processes are positive events. Remember that the survey has created an excellent opportunity for problem-solving communication.

Listen Carefully for the Real Feedback

We recall a company that received poor scores on a communications survey. The division management, eager to address communications issues, quickly started a company newsletter. The production was quite elaborate and included assigning a part-time person to the effort.

A year later, the company was preparing to repeat its survey and held a meeting that included some employees who had taken the survey the prior year. The group was reviewing the successes and shortcomings of the prior year's survey when a discussion arose around the company newsletter.

"The newsletter is good, but it still doesn't get the job done."

"Yeah," agreed another. There were general nods all around. The frustration of the human resource people was obvious, and one of them asked, "What would you say is wrong with it?"

"There's nothing wrong with it. It just isn't what people wanted. I think most of us were just talking about getting some bulletin boards for the hallways."

The moral of the story is to make sure you understand the requests that surface during feedback. Why do a lot when just a little would do more?

What Are Some Tips for Action Planning?

Allow time for brainstorming during the initial feedback meeting. Many organizations schedule one or two action planning sessions for follow-up, typically held about two weeks apart to give people time to reflect and absorb survey information. Once all the issues are discussed, whether in one meeting or several, we recommend that participants select two priorities: one will be an internal issue and the other an external issue.

Internal issues are defined as those that can be addressed within the work unit, though they may require approval from others. These can be initiated, assigned, and carried out by the "people in the room." We recommend that each work group identify just one or two internal action plans.

External issues are defined as those that have to be initiated, assigned, or carried out by others. We recommend that each work group limit itself to only one external issue. This is shared with the next level of management or another work group. As issues are passed up to the next level of management, they can choose to fix the identified issue or pass it up further to their management.

We do not recommend taking on more than three active issues at any one time. Each group documents its commitment to changing the one issue identified and provides timetables, responsibilities, and resources. The Rule of Two (or Three) has definite advantages. First, the survey will not result in the delivery of an excessive number of department requests to the senior executive. Instead, you will have a short list of true organizationwide problems and a series of specific actions taking place within work groups. The change efforts based on this approach are more easily executed, and employees have direct input into the solutions, which promotes organization-wide buy-in. Efforts are ultimately prioritized, and numerous changes are not going on all at once. Working together as a group to resolve issues helps build teamwork and supports the concept that progress is an "us" thing, not a "management" thing.

There is another benefit too. Generally, when multiple departments or work groups pass the same basic issues up to higher levels of management, those issues are in fact management issues.

Epilogue

SPEED COUNTS when you suspect an organizational difficulty. This book aims to speed your search for the questionnaires that will address these important organizational situations. The questionnaires in this book were designed to give you fast access to the reliable survey instruments you need.

In real-life organizational research, it matters how you ask. The number and order of questions can make a difference in survey outcome. The items in this book have all been used with other organizations, giving you confidence that they have helped others obtain the answers they needed when the occasions arose. As you've seen, you can use these questionnaires as a ready-made resource or as a source of guidance that helps you develop your own questions.

When you use these questionnaires for the first time, you have the opportunity to create a benchmark for your own organization. After several repeated administrations, you'll have the basis for internal norms. In the meantime, this book provides norms for thirty of the most important questions that appear on most employee morale surveys.

This book was designed for repeated reference. When you wonder what questions will reveal employees' beliefs about ethics in your organization, or you wonder how to inquire about fairness, or need the right words to probe for issues of management effectiveness, the questionnaires are there to help. We have covered twenty topics that organizations study the most frequently in our experience. Use the decision grid offered in Chapter Three to identify the right questionnaires for your situation.

In addition, the book covers some important supporting topics such as presurvey communications, questionnaire development, interpretation, and feedback in question-and-answer format.

If you need a fuller guide to the employee survey process and questionnaire items, see our earlier book, *The Employee Survey Package,* a two-volume set with more than 650 questionnaire items and complete survey process instructions. The norms offered in Chapter Two are current as of April 2004. Updates are available. Contact the authors for rates and information through surveys@performanceprograms.com or 1–800–565–4223.

We hope this resource brings you all the answers you need to understand attitude changes quickly and reliably.

Glossary

ANONYMITY. The survey respondent's identity is unknown to the survey sponsors.

AWARENESS CAMPAIGN. Advance communications that explain the survey to potential respondents.

CONFIDENTIALITY. Survey responses are not reported in any way that could lead to the identification of individuals through process of elimination or other means.

CONVENIENCE SAMPLE. A sample based on the data available to a researcher. In contrast, in a scientifically designed sample, the researcher defines the type of data required.

CUSTOMIZED QUESTIONNAIRES. Questionnaires written for a specific situation and using situation-specific language and concepts. Such questionnaires probably can be reused only within the same organization, if ever again.

FEEDBACK LEADERS. Typically department managers who will provide the results and gather reactions. With a small survey with a limited audience, the survey sponsor or spokesperson may also be the feedback leader.

FEEDBACK MEETINGS. Postsurvey meetings in which results are shared with the people who took the survey.

NORMS. Created by finding the average distribution of questionnaire responses for a large sample of survey respondents. They are a useful basis for comparison.

PRETESTING. Allowing potential respondents to react to the questionnaire or the awareness campaign materials before the survey.

QUESTIONNAIRE. The set of questions asked during a survey. Often used interchangeably with *survey*.

QUICK QUESTIONNAIRE. Our phrase for the short questionnaires supplied in this book. Because they are short and predesigned, they provide quick access to a usable question set.

STANDARD QUESTIONNAIRE. Questionnaires written for use "as is" in a broad assortment of situations.

STEERING TEAM. With formal, full-length employee surveys, a team typically chaired by the sponsor or spokesperson and directed by a human resource person acting as project manager. Steering team members might include cross-functional line management representatives from each division, as well as representatives of corporate and divisional human resources. Quick questionnaires may or may not require a steering team.

SURVEY. Used to describe either the entire survey process or just the questionnaire.

SURVEY PROJECT MANAGER. The individual responsible for managing the survey from initial goal development through postsurvey feedback.

SURVEY SPONSOR. The person with organizational responsibilities broad enough to take action on the survey results. He or she may or may not be the originator of the push to conduct the survey, but must embrace and promote it. Typically, survey sponsors are line managers with operational responsibilities.

About the Authors

Paul M. Connolly, Ph.D., has provided organizational measurement services since 1981, including employee surveys, 360-degree feedback, personality assessment, expatriate assessment, customer surveys, and stress management assessments. Connolly is the founder of Performance Programs, an organizational measurement firm in Old Saybrook, Connecticut. He has worked with organizations of all types, sizes, and locations, using multiple survey delivery and reporting methods. He has a B.A. from the College of the Holy Cross and an M.A. and Ph.D. from Fordham University. This is his fifth book in the human resource field.

Kathleen Groll Connolly has written a number of articles and three books on human resource topics. The most recent are *Employee Surveys: Practical and Proven Methods, Samples, Examples* and *The Employee Survey Question Guidebook.* She has held various marketing and management positions in both small and large businesses. She has a B.A. from Pennsylvania State University and an M.B.A. from New York University.

How to Use the CD-ROM

System Requirements

Windows PC

- 486 or Pentium processor-based personal computer
- Microsoft Windows 95 or Windows NT 3.51 or later
- Minimum RAM: 8MB for Windows 95 and NT
- Available space on hard disk: 8 MB Windows 95 and NT
- 2X speed CD-ROM drive or faster

Macintosh

- Macintosh with a 68020 or higher processor or Power Macintosh
- Apple OS version 7.0 or later
- Minimum RAM: 12MB for Macintosh
- Available space on hard disk: 6MB Macintosh
- 2X speed CD-ROM drive or faster

NOTE: This CD-ROM requires Netscape 3.0 or MS Internet Explorer 3.0 or higher.

Getting Started

Insert the CD-ROM into your drive. The CD-ROM will usually launch automatically. If it does not, click on the CD-ROM drive on your computer to launch. After you click to agree to the terms of the Copyright Page, the Home Page will appear.

Moving Around

Use the buttons at the left of each screen to move among the menu pages. To view a document listed on one of the menu pages, simply click on the name of the document. To quit a document at any time, click the box at the upper right-hand corner of the screen.

To quit the CD-ROM, you can click the Exit button or hit Alt-F4.

To Download Documents

Open the document you wish to download. Under the File pulldown menu, choose Save As. Save the document onto your hard drive with a different name. It is important to use a different name, otherwise the document may remain a read-only file.

You can also click on your CD drive in Windows Explorer and select a document to copy it to your hard drive and rename it.

In Case of Trouble

If you experience difficulty using this CD-ROM, please follow these steps:

1. Make sure your hardware and systems configurations conform to the systems requirements noted under "Systems Requirements" above.

2. Review the installation procedure for your type of hardware and operating system. It is possible to reinstall the software if necessary.

3. Have a question, comment, or suggestion? Contact us! We value your feedback, and we want to hear from you.

For questions about this or other Pfeiffer products, you may contact us by:

E-mail: customer@wiley.com

Mail: Customer Care Wiley/Pfeiffer
         10475 Crosspoint Blvd.
         Indianapolis, IN 46256

Phone: (U.S.) 800-274-4434 (Outside the U.S. 317-572-3985)

Fax: (U.S.) 800-569-0443 (Outside the U.S. 317-572-4002)

To order additional copies of this product or to browse other Pfeiffer products visit us online at www.pfeiffer.com.

To speak with someone in Product Technical Support, call 800-762-2974 or 317-572-3994 Monday through Friday 8:30 a.m. to 5 p.m. (EST). You can also contact Product Technical Support and get support information through our website at http://www.wiley.com/techsupport

Before calling or writing, please have the following information available:

- Type of operating system
- Any error messages displayed
- Complete description of the problem

It is best if you are sitting at your computer when making the call.

Pfeiffer Publications Guide

This guide is designed to familiarize you with the various types of Pfeiffer publications. The formats section describes the various types of products that we publish; the methodologies section describes the many different ways that content might be provided within a product. We also provide a list of the topic areas in which we publish.

FORMATS

In addition to its extensive book-publishing program, Pfeiffer offers content in an array of formats, from fieldbooks for the practitioner to complete, ready-to-use training packages that support group learning.

FIELDBOOK Designed to provide information and guidance to practitioners in the midst of action. Most fieldbooks are companions to another, sometimes earlier, work, from which its ideas are derived; the fieldbook makes practical what was theoretical in the original text. Fieldbooks can certainly be read from cover to cover. More likely, though, you'll find yourself bouncing around following a particular theme, or dipping in as the mood, and the situation, dictate.

HANDBOOK A contributed volume of work on a single topic, comprising an eclectic mix of ideas, case studies, and best practices sourced by practitioners and experts in the field.

An editor or team of editors usually is appointed to seek out contributors and to evaluate content for relevance to the topic. Think of a handbook not as a ready-to-eat meal, but as a cookbook of ingredients that enables you to create the most fitting experience for the occasion.

RESOURCE Materials designed to support group learning. They come in many forms: a complete, ready-to-use exercise (such as a game); a comprehensive resource on one topic (such as conflict management) containing a variety of methods and approaches; or a collection of like-minded activities (such as icebreakers) on multiple subjects and situations.

TRAINING PACKAGE An entire, ready-to-use learning program that focuses on a particular topic or skill. All packages comprise a guide for the facilitator/trainer and a workbook for the participants. Some packages are supported with additional media—such as video—or learning aids, instruments, or other devices to help participants understand concepts or practice and develop skills.

- *Facilitator/trainer's guide* Contains an introduction to the program, advice on how to organize and facilitate the learning event, and step-by-step instructor notes. The guide also contains copies of presentation materials—handouts, presentations, and overhead designs, for example—used in the program.

- *Participant's workbook* Contains exercises and reading materials that support the learning goal and serves as a valuable reference and support guide for participants in the weeks and months that follow the learning event. Typically, each participant will require his or her own workbook.

ELECTRONIC CD-ROMs and web-based products transform static Pfeiffer content into dynamic, interactive experiences. Designed to take advantage of the searchability, automation, and ease-of-use that technology provides, our e-products bring convenience and immediate accessibility to your workspace.

METHODOLOGIES

CASE STUDY A presentation, in narrative form, of an actual event that has occurred inside an organization. Case studies are not prescriptive, nor are they used to prove a point; they are designed to develop critical analysis and decision-making skills. A case study has a specific time frame, specifies a sequence of events, is narrative in structure, and contains a plot structure—an issue (what should be/have been done?). Use case studies when the goal is to enable participants to apply previously learned theories to the circumstances in the case, decide what is pertinent, identify the real issues, decide what should have been done, and develop a plan of action.

ENERGIZER A short activity that develops readiness for the next session or learning event. Energizers are most commonly used after a break or lunch to stimulate or refocus the group. Many involve some form of physical activity, so they are a useful way to counter post-lunch lethargy. Other uses include transitioning from one topic to another, where "mental" distancing is important.

EXPERIENTIAL LEARNING ACTIVITY (ELA) A facilitator-led intervention that moves participants through the learning cycle from experience to application (also known as a Structured Experience). ELAs are carefully thought-out designs in which there is a definite learning purpose and intended outcome. Each step—everything that participants do during the activity—facilitates the accomplishment of the stated goal. Each ELA includes complete instructions for facilitating the intervention and a clear statement of goals, suggested group size and timing, materials required, an explanation of the process, and, where appropriate, possible variations to the activity. (For more detail on Experiential Learning Activities, see the Introduction to the *Reference Guide to Handbooks and Annuals*, 1999 edition, Pfeiffer, San Francisco.)

GAME A group activity that has the purpose of fostering team spirit and togetherness in addition to the achievement of a pre-stated goal. Usually contrived—undertaking a desert expedition, for example—this type of learning method offers an engaging means for participants to demonstrate and practice business and interpersonal skills. Games are effective for team building and personal development mainly because the goal is subordinate to the process—the means through which participants reach decisions, collaborate, communicate, and generate trust and understanding. Games often engage teams in "friendly" competition.

ICEBREAKER A (usually) short activity designed to help participants overcome initial anxiety in a training session and/or to acquaint the participants with one another. An icebreaker can be a fun activity or can be tied to specific topics or training goals. While a useful tool in itself, the icebreaker comes into its own in situations where tension or resistance exists within a group.

INSTRUMENT A device used to assess, appraise, evaluate, describe, classify, and summarize various aspects of human behavior. The term used to describe an instrument depends primarily on its format and purpose. These terms include survey, questionnaire, inventory, diagnostic, survey, and poll. Some uses of instruments include providing instrumental feedback to group members, studying here-and-now processes or functioning within a group, manipulating group composition, and evaluating outcomes of training and other interventions.

Instruments are popular in the training and HR field because, in general, more growth can occur if an individual is provided with a method for focusing specifically on his or her own behavior. Instruments also are used to obtain information that will serve as a basis for change and to assist in workforce planning efforts.

Paper-and-pencil tests still dominate the instrument landscape with a typical package comprising a facilitator's guide, which offers advice on administering the instrument and interpreting the collected data, and an initial set of instruments. Additional instruments are available separately. Pfeiffer, though, is investing heavily in e-instruments. Electronic instrumentation provides effortless distribution and, for larger groups particularly, offers advantages over paper-and-pencil tests in the time it takes to analyze data and provide feedback.

LECTURETTE A short talk that provides an explanation of a principle, model, or process that is pertinent to the participants' current learning needs. A lecturette is intended to establish a common language bond between the trainer and the participants by providing a mutual frame of reference. Use a lecturette as an introduction to a group activity or event, as an interjection during an event, or as a handout.

MODEL A graphic depiction of a system or process and the relationship among its elements. Models provide a frame of reference and something more tangible, and more easily remembered, than a verbal explanation. They also give participants something to "go on," enabling them to track their own progress as they experience the dynamics, processes, and relationships being depicted in the model.

ROLE PLAY A technique in which people assume a role in a situation/scenario: a customer service rep in an angry-customer exchange, for example. The way in which the role is approached is then discussed and feedback is offered. The role play is often repeated using a different approach and/or incorporating changes made based on feedback received. In other words, role playing is a spontaneous interaction involving realistic behavior under artificial (and safe) conditions.

SIMULATION A methodology for understanding the interrelationships among components of a system or process. Simulations differ from games in that they test or use a model that depicts or mirrors some aspect of reality in form, if not necessarily in content. Learning occurs by studying the effects of change on one or more factors of the model. Simulations are commonly used to test hypotheses about what happens in a system—often referred to as "what if?" analysis—or to examine best-case/worst-case scenarios.

THEORY A presentation of an idea from a conjectural perspective. Theories are useful because they encourage us to examine behavior and phenomena through a different lens.

TOPICS

The twin goals of providing effective and practical solutions for workforce training and organization development and meeting the educational needs of training and human resource professionals shape Pfeiffer's publishing program. Core topics include the following:

Leadership & Management

Communication & Presentation

Coaching & Mentoring

Training & Development

E-Learning

Teams & Collaboration

OD & Strategic Planning

Human Resources

Consulting

What will you find on pfeiffer.com?

- The best in workplace performance solutions for training and HR professionals

- Downloadable training tools, exercises, and content

- Web-exclusive offers

- Training tips, articles, and news

- Seamless on-line ordering

- Author guidelines, information on becoming a Pfeiffer Affiliate, and much more

Discover more at www.pfeiffer.com

Customer Care

Have a question, comment, or suggestion? Contact us! We value your feedback and we want to hear from you.

For questions about this or other Pfeiffer products, you may contact us by:

E-mail: **customer@wiley.com**

Mail: **Customer Care Wiley/Pfeiffer**
10475 Crosspoint Blvd.
Indianapolis, IN 46256

Phone: **(US) 800-274-4434** (Outside the US: 317-572-3985)

Fax: **(US) 800-569-0443** (Outside the US: 317-572-4002)

To order additional copies of this title or to browse other Pfeiffer products, visit us online at **www.pfeiffer.com**.

For **Technical Support** questions call **(800) 274-4434**.

For authors guidelines, log on to www.pfeiffer.com and click on "Resources for Authors."

If you are . . .

A **college bookstore, a professor, an instructor, or work in higher education** and you'd like to place an order or request an exam copy, please contact jbreview@wiley.com.

A **general retail bookseller** and you'd like to establish an account or speak to a local sales representative, contact Melissa Grecco at 201-748-6267 or mgrecco@wiley.com.

An **exclusively on-line bookseller**, contact Amy Blanchard at 530-756-9456 or ablanchard @wiley.com or Jennifer Johnson at 206-568-3883 or jjohnson@wiley.com, both of our Online Sales department.

A **librarian or library representative**, contact John Chambers in our Library Sales department at 201-748-6291 or jchamber@wiley.com.

A **reseller, training company/consultant, or corporate trainer**, contact Charles Regan in our Special Sales department at 201-748-6553 or cregan@wiley.com.

A **specialty retail distributor** (includes specialty gift stores, museum shops, and corporate bulk sales), contact Kim Hendrickson in our Special Sales department at 201-748-6037 or khendric@wiley.com.

Purchasing for the **Federal government**, contact Ron Cunningham in our Special Sales department at 317-572-3053 or rcunning@wiley.com.

Purchasing for a **State or Local government**, contact Charles Regan in our Special Sales department at 201-748-6553 or cregan@wiley.com.